WOMEN IN POLITICS

Edited by
Dr. Dasarathi Bhuyan
Lecturer Political Science
Bellaguntha Science College
Dist. Ganjam – 761 119
Orissa (India)

DISCOVERY PUBLISHING HOUSE PVT. LTD.
NEW DELHI-110 002

First Published-2008
Reprinted: 2013
ISBN 978-81-8356-346-8

Published by:
DISCOVERY PUBLISHING HOUSE PVT. LTD.
4831/24, Ansari Road, Prahlad Street
Darya Ganj, New Delhi-110002 (India)
Phone: 23279245 • Fax: 91-11-23253475
E-mail: dphbooks@rediffmail.com
dphtemp@indiatimes.com
website: www.discoverypublishinghouse.com

Printed at:
Dynamic Printers, Delhi

PREFACE

Women politics is the least researched topics in our country. It is as neglected as the women are in the Indian society. For a long time the social scientists did not throw a firm look at the political behaviour of women. It was partially owing to the backwardness of behavioural research in India. However, the more significant aspect accountable for the scarcity of women studies is the lack of due weight accorded to the women in the society. Even today women studies are very few in number and women politics as a field of research is still in its budding stage. The current study is an attempt to fill up this vacuum and throw light on the political behaviour of women.

Women comprise about 50 per cent of country's population. However, they are the biggest debarred group roughly in all facets. The male is denying their rights and liberties. Due to the male domination of Indian society, their social, economic and political status has stayed behind comparatively stumpy. From the time immemorial, they have been classified in all activity of life and regarded as "second class citizen".

In every field, men have steadily subjugated them. The subjugation of women by men is not confined only to developed countries; this is also present though to a lesser degree in most developing countries like India. The phase of growth of a country is enormously connected with the status of women in their country. The socio-economic status of a woman is liable to affect her political participation.

The present socio-economic status of Indian women is not favourable for the successful involvement in political affairs. Women are politically not dynamic and do not offer to involve herself in the public affairs. Political equality is meaningless without social and economic equality. Aside from these, women experiences from traditional attitudes, which made them to be aware of that they are unequal. A better social, economic and political condition of women is indispensable for political involvement. Those who have powers, material knowledge, resources are in a position to involve in the decision making process.

Unless women become the equal allies of development, the country cannot flourish. Comprehending the significance of women welfare, the founding fathers of Indian constitution have made special provisions in the constitution to guarantee women's rights and gender equality. The 73rd Constitutional Amendment Act of 1992-93 opened a new chapter in the history of democratic decentralisation in India by transferring power to the people and giving a chance to womenfolk to utter their right to be heard in the decision making process. Reservation has also led to the recognition of the identity of women and their presence in the public life. This is a significant change from the earlier perception. It is also observed that there is an increase of women's power at the grass root level. Women have started emphasizing themselves as a vital weapon for social change. In future the Implementation of women's reservation bill that desires guaranteeing 33 per cent reservation in Parliament and State Legislatures will bring about a revolution in our country.

Actually, the constitutional provisions have not been materialised into reality. On the other hand it has been noticed that the elected women representatives are treated 'as puppet' in the local bodies. The majorities of them stay silent audience to the events of the Gram Panchayat meetings and seldom take part in the deliberations. They hardly say their own view relating to identifying beneficiaries, assigning contracts, locating developmental projects, budget preparation, planning etc. Just sitting and listening the meeting have been their style of involvement. The reasons that distressing the route of women empowerment and participation are identified as lack of awareness, experience, knowledge, skill, leadership quality, low level of education, lack of exposure, influence of family, caste, social outlook, patriarch etc. Illiteracy has become a major obstacle in the path of playing active role in the functioning of local bodies. The Indian male community until today considers that the profession of women is to "cook and serve; ruling the mass is not their work, it is men's special licence."

Husbands and family members do not want their women representatives to interact with government officials and others in matter of taking decisions. The caste factor is one more check in the route of women participation. Higher caste people like the Brahmins and Khyatriyas are hesitant to honour the low caste elected women representative and to obey decisions taken by a low caste leader. In this way, they are confronting innumerable complicatedness, nuisance and disgrace at the hands of traditional power holders (high caste groups).

Women's involvement in decision-making process will show the way to the progress of standards of public life. Occurrence of rape, molestation, dowry killing, female infanticide and domestic violence against women are increasing in alarming proportions due to the low standard of women in society. By politically empowering women, this can surely be evaded. Awareness campaign should be created in support of women empowerment. Mass media, Non Governmental Organisations, Political Parties Self Help Group's (S.H.Gs), Mahila Mandals have an important responsibility to create awareness about the importance of political empowerment of women. The 21st century in particular promoted the cause of gender justice by internationalising struggles for equality by women and other oppressed people. Thc question of political participation of women in India in a dynamic manner deserves attention. To materialise these dreams into reality an attempt has been made in this volume in form of comprehensive discussions to generate awareness for political empowerment of women. This volume contains highly research-oriented articles contributed by social scientists, researchers, professors and academicians. I am enormously grateful to all the contributors for their kind cooperation, unfathomable trust and faith on me.

My sincere gratitude is due also to the proprietor, Discovery Publishing House, New Delhi, who extended me unmitigated support and cooperation for publishing this volume. I am sure that the book will full ensure the academic needs of the researchers, scholars, readers, social activists, political decision makers and women activists busy in politics.

Dr. Dasarathi Bhuyan
Editor

CONTENTS

1

WOMEN IN PANCHAYATI RAJ INSTITUTIONS

A CASE STUDY IN ORISSA

Dr. JAYANTA PARIDA*

This paper studies the role and performance of elected women representatives in the functioning of Gram Panchayat in Aul block in Orissa. It finds that due to the provisions of 73rd Constitutional Amendment Act, a new set of women representatives come into Gram Panchayat. Reservation (affirmative action) has created a space for women's needs within the structural framework of politics and legitimised women issues. But the affirmative action in form of reservation has not been successful in ensuring "proper and effective representation" of women. Despite reservation, the power equations have not changed in the rural society.

Women constitute about 50 per cent of country's population. But they are the largest excluded category in almost all aspects. They have been denied to their rights and liberties by the male dominated Indian society for which their social, economic and political status has remained relatively low. For centuries they have been discriminated in all walks of life and treated as "second class citizen".

* **Lecturer in Political Science, Bhadrak Junior College, Bhadrak, Orissa – 756 100.**

Women's development has, therefore, been one of the major issues in India. Right from independence' gender discrimination has been identified as one of the most serious issues. After independence, it was realised by the policy makers that unless women become the equal partners of development, the country can not prosper. Realising the importance of women welfare, the founding fathers of Indian constitution have made special provisions in the constitution to ensure women's rights and gender equality. In the constitution, gender equality is enshrined in the Preamble, Fundamental Rights, Fundamental Duties, and Directive Principles of State Policy. The constitution not only grants equal status to women but also empowers the state to adopt measures for positive discrimination in favour of women. Since independence the has enacted many women specific legislations to safeguard women's rights. In all the five year plans emphasis has been placed to raise the socoio-economic status of women.

The question of women's representation in politics in all over the world began to assume importance since 1975 when United Nations declared the decade as the "Women Development Decade" and adopted some resolutions for women's empowerment. The Nairobi Conference 1985 called on the participating nations to take steps for ensuing women participation in politics through reservation of 35 per cent seats in election.

However, in India the equation of women's participation in politics through Panchayati Raj institutions got the attention of the Committee on the Status of Women in India (1974). But the concept of statutory all women Panchayats which it suggested, has not been very effective. The National Perspective Plan for Women (1988) has also argued that political power and access to decision making process are critical prerequisites for women's equality in the process of national –building. The committee pleaded for women's participation in all rural local-self governing bodies. But the 73rd Constitutional Amendment Act, 1993 may be regarded as a watershed in the history of state's initiative in regards to political empowerment and participation of rural women. The 73rd Constitutional Amendment Act has opened up the windows of opportunities for women to emerge as leaders and play an effective role in the grass root bodies. This Amendment Act provides one-third reservation of seats for women in Panchayati Raj institutions along with reservation of seats for SCs and STs Women. It also provides for the reservation of one-third of total number of offices of chairpersons in the Panchayats at all the levels for women. Further, the Orissa Panchayati Raj Act, 1991 provides that if the chairperson post is held by a male member, the vice-chairperson seat will be occupied by a woman member.

Purpose and Methodology of the Study

The 73rd Constitutional Amendment Act ,1993 opened a new chapter in the history of democratic decentralisation in India by devolving power to the people and given opportunities to women folk to express their voice in the decision making process. But how far have the constitutional provisions been translated into reality? In order to asses the effectiveness of political empowerment and level of political participation of rural women, the present micro study was carried out at Aul (Aali) block of Kendrapara District of Orissa. The main of the study are:

(i) To assess the performance and level of participation of elected women representatives in the functioning of Panchayats;

(ii) To identify the factors affecting the performance of women representatives in the village decision making process; and

(iii) To suggest measures for making the process of participation of women real and effective in the Panchayati Raj bodies.

The empirical data for the study have been collected from the Aul block, which consists of 32 Gram Panchayats. In order to document the level of participation and performance of the elected women representatives in the functioning of Panchaysats, a combination of interview method and focused group discussions was used for the study . In total 60 elected women representatives (8 Sarpanches, 10 vice-sarpanches and 42 ward members) have been interviewed and their responses regarding their participation and performance in grass root bodies are found both positive and negatives.

On the positive side it has been noticed that due to reservation of seats many women were elected to local bodies. Reservation has created a space for women's needs within the structural framework of politics and legitimised women's issue. The women to feel happy and energetic being placed at the mainstream of the society and given opportunity to share power with men. Reservation has also led to the recognition of the identity of women and their presence in the public life. This is a remarkable change from the earlier perception. It is also noticed that there is an upsurge of women's power at the grassroot bodies. Women have started asserting themselves leading to a new kind of social revolution in the society. Some of the women representatives are slowly and steadily gaining confidence and trying to perceive their roles by familiarising themselves with Panchayat rules and regulations.

On the negative side it has been found that the elected women representatives are treated 'as puppet' in the Panchayats . Most of them remain silent spectators to the proceedings of the Gram Panchayat meetings and rarely participate in the discussions. They hardly voice their own opinion regarding identifying beneficiaries' assigning contracts, locating developmental projects etc. Simply sitting and listening to proceedings of the meeting have been their form of participation. Active participation in the form of involving in the decision making process, budget preparation, planning etc, was found to be rare in case of women representatives. Due to male dominance, elected women members are functioning more or less as dummies –the husbands of women Sarpanches are actively participating in the Panchayat matters instead of allowing their wives to take part in the decision making process. Financial matters are not tackled by the women representatives and for this they depend upon their husbands or sons or any other male relatives. Practically it has been found that two heads are functioning at Gram Panchayat levels—she head (de-jure)—the elected women Sarpanch and he head (de-facto)—the real Sarpanch. Most of the elected women Sarpanches are regarded as a mere 'Rubber Stamp' and all the functions of the Panchayat are being performed by their husbands or local elites.

Attendance of elected women representatives in Gram Panchayat meeting is found very low. Majority of them did not attend the meeting regularly. In spite of reservation of seats for women, the meetings of the Gram Panchayat are overwhelmingly a male dominated event. Gender differences are observed with regard to raising problems of the area in Panchayat meetings. None of the women representatives choose to raise the problems of their locality frequently. Capacity to raise issues in the Panchayat meetings is found to be low among the women representatives. It is found that women representatives are taking the help of male members to make their explicit in Panchayat meetings. In most of the cases women representatives prferred to tell the Sarpanch or any member in advance about the problems. They are also observed discussing with the Sarapanches after the meeting. The reason for this was shyness and nervousness of the women in talking in front of others, particularly in front of male representatives.

It is observed that many factors are affecting the process of participation and level of performance of women in the grass roots' bodies. These factors may be categorised as of two types: (i) Internal Factor; and (ii) External Factor. The internal factors which affecting the process of women empowerment and participation are identified as: lack of awareness, experience, knowledge, skill, leadership quality, low level of education, lack of exposure etc. It is noticed that women representatives are not aware of their functions, duties and responsibilities. In fact, they do not know what role they have to play in the functioning of local government. Lack of education or low level of education has become a major obstacle in the path of playing active role in the functioning of Panchayats. The elected members are unable to understand the basic of working of Gram Panchayats. As a result they provide an ineffective leadership. Due to lack of exposure and experience, women members in several cases are dependent on their husbands in the matter of decision making. In many cases they do rely upon the traditional power holders.

The external factors which affect the process of participation and empowerment of women are: influence of family, caste, social outlook, patriarchy etc. The dominated Indian society does not perceive women as capable or worthy of leadership. The Indian males still perceive that they are alone capable of occupying positions and holding power. On one occasion one elected male representatives remarked "what do the women folk now? Their job is to cook and serve; governance is not their job, it is our exclusive privilege." Patriarchal influences and traditional norms of our society hinder the path of women empowerment in the local government.

Another important stumbling block on the way of women empowerment is family influence. Many family members do not want that their women members should participate in the village meetings. They do not allow their elected women representatives to interact with government officials and others in the matter of taking decisions. They are cases, where the husband opposed their wives active participation in local politics. The influence of casteism is also found to be another constraint in the process of women participation. It was noticed that upper caste people are either hesitant or unwilling to honour or implement decisions taken by a scheduled caste women leaders. Traditional and cultural norms of the society undermine the functioning of the schedule caste women representatives in the grass root bodies. These women representatives were facing a lot of difficulties, harassment and humiliation at the hands of upper caste people and traditional power holders.

Conclusion

From the above analysis we may conclude that reservation (affirmative action) has resulted in bringing a new set of women representative in to Gram Panchayats . But the affirmative action in form of decentralisation has not been successful in ensuring "proper and effective representation of women". This is with respect to participation of women in the functioning of Panchayats and their responses towards citizen's interests in the local government. The involvement of women representative in the decision making process is not effective and husbands to women and other local elites minimise women representative role in the Panchayats by exerting control over them and acting as de facto member, Despite affirmative action the power equations have not changed in the rural society.

However, women representatives has ample scope for involvement in the process of local governments. To make their participation real and effective there urgent need to change traditional social attitude and patriarchal values of society. There is also need for positive attitudinal change and mental make-up of the male folk in favor of women participation.

Since the rural women representatives are lacking in knowledge, self-confidence and skill, they should be given appropriate training to improve their knowledge base and capacity level relating to their rights, responsibilities and duties in the functioning of Panchayat bodies. They should be made acquainted with the procedures of Gram Panchayat rules, regulations and financial management. There is also need for launching more and more awareness campaigns in favour of women empowerment. Mass media, NGOs, Political Parties, Self Help Group's (SHGs), Mahila Mandals have a significant role to play to sensitise civil society and generate awareness about the importance of women empowerment so that the process of political participation of women will be real and increasingly affective.

REFERENCES

Dutta, P., (1998), *Major Issues in the Development Debate—Lessons in Empowerment in India*, Kaniska, New Delhi.

Fraser A, (1993): *Women and Public Life, Minneapolis, WRAW.*

Ghatak, M and M.Ghatak(2002): "Recent Reforms in the Panchayat System in West Bengal: Towards Greater Participatory Governance?", *EPW*, Vol. 37(I), pp. 45-48.

Institute of Social-Economic Development (1998): *Assigning the Participation of Women in Local Governance—Exploring New Frontiers: Orissa Experience*, ISED, and Bhubaneswar.

Karl, M, (1995) *Women and Empowerment: Participation in Decision Making*, Zed Books, London.

Kotvi, M.S. (1999) *Empowerment of Women: Gender Equity* — A Myth, in Journal of Constitutional and Parliamentary Studies, Institute of Constitutional and Parliamentary Studies, New Delhi, pp. 134-139.

Mishra, R., (1998): "Devolution Power to Women in Panchayati Raj in Orissa: Challenges and Opportunities", *Kurukshetra*, New Delhi, Vol. 47(2), pp. 19-24.

Murty, R.K. (eds.) (2001), *"Building Women's Capacities: Intervention in Gender Transformation"*. Sage, New Delhi.

Narasimhan, S. (1999), Empowering Rural Women: An Over View, *Kurukshetra*, Vol. 47, No. 12.

National Policy for Empowerment of Women (2001), Department of Women and Child Development, Government of India , New Delhi.

Panda, S. (1999): Political Empowerment of Women: Case of Orissa PRIs; *Indian Journal of Public Administration*, Vol. 45(I) , pp. 86-93.

Patanaik, P, (2005): "Affirmative Action and Representation of Weaker Sections", *Economic and Political Weekly*, October, 29, pp. 4753-4761.

Peerzade, S.A. and Parande, P. (2005), Empowerment of Women: A Study; Kurukshetra, Vol. 54, No. 1.

Seth, M. (2001), *Women and Development: The Indian Experiences*, Sage, New Delhi.

Squires, J. (1999): Rethinking and Boundaries of Political Representation' in Sylvia, W. (ed). *New Agenda for Women*, Macmillan, London.

2

POLITICAL PARTICIPATION OF WOMEN IN THE POLITICAL PROCESS IN ASSAM

AN INTROSPECTION

SWAPNA NEOGI*

Abstract

In the eastern most corner of India situated the North Eastern Region of which Assam is one of the eight states of the region. Though Assam is full of natural and mineral resources it is mainly an agro-based state. 80 per cent of it populace reside in village areas and mostly agriculturists.

Women constitute half of the total population of the state. Most of them are busy with their household affairs. They also contribute economically to their respective family helping their counterparts in fields, supporting them by bearing and rearing children. The social status of women of Assam is far better than the other states in India as Rajasthan, Uttar Pradesh, and Punjab where injustice to women is a common practice, for instance, in matters of dowry system.

* **Department of Political Science, Dhing College, Dhing, Nagaon-782123 (Assam).**

In tribal areas of Assam the Boro, Karbi, Lalung, Dimasa, Rabha, Garo, Kuki, Hajong, Deuri etc. the status of women is fairly good. They have their distinct identity with different attires and dialects. Generally they work in fields and also perform other household activities like fishing, collection of firewood, weaving. About 90 per cent women are performing household affairs and the rest engage in governmental and the other sectors as employees. Nearly 80 per cent women are illiterate in tribal areas of Assam.

The tea communities in Assam constitute almost a million tea workers out of which 50 per cent are women working as tea labourers in tea industries. Almost 90 per cent of them are lacking even formal education and their standard of living is extremely deplorable.

All those above-mentioned communities altogether constitute the Assamese society. Though in most the societies the social and economic status of women have largely improved, their political status needs a thorough analysis.

In this paper, it is attempted to discuss about women participation in political process in Assam, just an overall view.

Since the last two decades historic attempts have been initiated by the government through a few unique legislations but has failed to exert any reckonable impact on women which is crystal clear from results of periodic elections both in the national and in the state of Assam along with other states in India although women representation in grass root level institutions have considerably increased than it was before.

Introduction

In the helm of all living beings there are two separate and opposite ingredients, male and female and that is that the biological adjustment, the law of nature, the broad-base of all living creatures of the universe rotate around. Society of human being is one of the unit of the whole component of that cosmology.

Female make up 50 per cent of the entire population throughout the world. But their participation in political life is very nominal. Both in local and in national spectrum women participation in Indian polity is still marginally at lower level even after 60 years of India's independence. Assam is having a very miserable standing in matters of women representation in the state political arena. Though election was first held in Assam in 1937 just after acquiring by it the category of a full-fledged state in 1921, consciousness of women as regards their political rights is still to gear up.

Assam is situated between the latitude of 24° to 28° N and approximately from longitude 90° to 97° E and it is at 795 meters above the sea level. Assam has a total landed area of 78,438 square kilometers along with a total number of populations of 2,66,55,528. Male populace coving 1,37,77,037 and female population consists of 1,28,78,491. The sex ratio shows against per 1000 male there are 932 female and the percentage is 51.78 per cent male and 48.22 per cent female (Census Report: 2001).

The condition of women in ancient Assam was considerably good when they led a respectable life at home and in the society. They were provided with certain types of education too.

During the medieval period, more specially during the Ahom period Assam had produced a handful of gallant and efficient women namely, warriors like Mulagabharu, Radha Rukmini; administrators like Phuleshwari, Sarbeswari, Ambika; diplomats as Kuranganayani, Pijou, Ramani Gabharu. In this period women served the society in all spheres, social economic, political in various capacities as weavers, dancers in temples, administrators, spies.

During feudal period the role and the status of women was very miserable in Assam like that of other parts of India. On the precept of religious norms and faith they were kept captivated inside home entirely depriving them of right and liberty, respect and dignity.

However, their condition drastically changed in time of the British period, the beginning of the modern age in Assam. Few British administrators along with few social reformists of India of the moderate group could turn the society into a more scientific and rational one by abolishing such prejudices as 'Sati', 'Child Marriage' which carried indelible influences in the Assamese society. During this period women were sent to schools. The familial, social and legal status of women comparatively improved during this period.

Sacrifices that had been made by the Indian women in the struggle for independence of the country is still written in golden letters in the pages of history of India like Sarojini Naidu, Vijoya Laxmi Pandit, Katurba Gandhi. The role played by the women of Assam in time of the freedom movement reminds us of their sacrifices, courage and patriotic commitment for the cause of the locality in particular and the nation in general. Eminent women like Hemoprava Das, Chadraprava Saikiani, Guneswari Devi, Amal Prava Das, Pushpalata Das are mentioned worthy. It was also for their utmost efforts, socio-economic cultural-religious behaviour of the Assamese society radically changed in later periods in Assam.

After independence, in India, we have the system of democratic set-up with liberal principles as the broad base of the nation's philosophy in all areas of activity under such a principle the destiny of women has begun to alter from male domination to greater emancipation. With the constitutional rights along with number of legislations promoted move specially the elite women group in Assam to accept positive attitude towards their life. Their gradual realisation of possession of qualitative values and being as individual also has changed their status of an *'abala'*(a weak), helpless and powerless person into a human being having equal power, role and status in the society.

The United Nation Declaration of 1975 as 'Women's Year' and the next decade as 'Women's Decade', the Forth Women Conference of Beijing in 1995 also changed the condition of women with the initiative of government taking some measures directed to improve women's status in the faminial, social, legal and political matters.

But it is precise to note that we have yet to run a long race to reach to the expectation, which necessitates sincerity of purpose adorned with determination on the part of the government, political parties, to minimise the gap between male/female, the self-imposed social bondage of human race called gender-discrimination.

This paper focuses on women in political process in Assam, an overall elucidation.

However, it is a truism that despite of manifold constrains, women have come out from their houses and engaged themselves in all sectors of outdoor activities. We are having the first ever woman President of India Srimati Pratiba Patil and down in the rank those labourers even in remote areas and the same picture is in view in case of Assam too. In Assam we could see Srimati Anowara Taimur, the first ever woman Chief Minister and women workforce scattered in all other fronts of activity in the state.

Methodology

Both primary and secondary data's were used for analysis of women participation in polity of Assam and reference had been made on few important issues concerning the nation-India since the first elections held in 1952 both for Parliament and for Assam State Legislative Assembly. Secondary datas had been collected from published materials particularly Census Reports, State Statistical Reports, Books, Journals, Newspapers, Election Branch, Office of the Deputy Commissioner, Nagaon, Assam, Office of the Deputy Director, Economic and Statics Nagaon, Assam. Interviews had also been conducted where it was found necessary.

Objectives

The paper addresses itself to the state of representation of women in the Indian Parliament and in Assam State Legislative Assembly along with a few statistical datas relating other nations of the world. The specific objective of the study is to find out the growth rate of female electors turned out during periodic elections, the economic, social and more importantly the political status of women specifically in Assam indicating female populace of the state. It has been also tried to highlight constrains women have been facing regarding their active participation in the political life in the state.

The finding of the study would be used to suggest few points as realised for awareness and active involvement of womenfolk in the process of polity of the nation in general and the state of Assam in particular.

Findings of the Study

The entire population of Assam is constituted by 50 per cent of female populace but their representation both in the national as well as in the state levels reveals a dismal picture. So far the world scenario is concerned the percentage is to some extend higher. In Germany, Argentina, South Africa women representatives cover in-between 25 per cent to 29 per cent of the total number of representatives in Parliament. Sweden is at the top having 40 per cent of women representatives in the polity of the nation.

In India the percentage of women representatives in the Lok Sabha as against the total number of seats has been marginally very low. In 1952 it was 4.4 per cent, in 1957, 5.4 per cent, in 1962 6.7 per cent and only in 1991 women percentage of representation increased to 7 per cent and never gone beyond 8 per cent till date (The Assam Tribune, February 15, 2007).

In Assam along with other states of India in the State Legislative Assemblies of the nation, the average percentage of women representation is yet to touch the figure of 10 per cent (The Assam Tribune, February 15, 2007).

But there has been an elaborate constitutional arrangement providing women with equal rights. Articles 15,16 denounce discrimination and inequality in any form both in case of man and woman. Under Article 51A(c) it is declared that it is the duty of every citizen of India to 'renounce practice derogatory to the dignity of women'. Under Articles 325 and 326, women are not only given voting rights but also equal rights in matters of election. Chapter IV comprising of Directive Principles of State Policy and certain directives are specially meant for emancipation of women. Article 39 provides for 'equal pay for equal work irrespective of sex.'

But in spite of all such constitutional rights provided for women, they are yet to fully understand their practical values resulting in certain constrains in the process of developing a matured political behaviour on their part.

Followings are a number of Tables showing the picture of women participation in the political process of India and Assam, their growth rate as electors' in Assam and their rate of percentage.

Table 2.1

Women from Assam contested for the Lok Sabha seat in General Election and returned

Year of Election Held	*No. of Women Candidate Contested*	*No. or Women Candidate Returned*
1952	2	1
1957	2	2
1962	3	2
1967	1	1
1971	3	1
1977	3	1
1980	2	Nil
1983	...	...
1985	3	Nil
1991	5	Nil
1996	9	Nil
1998	3	1
2004	6	Nil

Source: Compiled from the book, Women of Assam (1952-1991), pp. 76 and Election Branch, Office of the Deputy Commissioner Nagaon, Assam.)

Thus, since 1952 up to the last General Election in 2004, Women have had failed to adequately represent Assam and the number of representatives are very few. Srimati Bonily Khongmen was the first women representative in the Lok Sabha from Assam, (1952). In the Rajya Sabha also we had a few women representatives namely, Pushpalata Das, (Cong.), Srimati Vijya Chakravaty (AGP), Srimati Anawara Taimur (Cong.), Srimati Jayashree Goswami Mahanta (AGP).

Table 2.2

No. of women contested for the state legislative assembly seats and returned

Year of Election Held Candidate	*No. of Women Candidate Returned*	*No. of Women Contested*
1952	5	1
1957	7	5
1962	4	4
1967	8	5
1972	10	8
1978	215	21
1983	2	2
1985	18	3
1991	18	3
1996	45	5
2001	–	(not available)
2006	70	14

Source: Women of Assam, pp. 76, (1952-1991) and Election Branch, Nagaon Deputy Commissioner's Office, 1996-2006).

From the above analysis it has come to light that the women representation is exceedingly less in member.

Table 2.3

Turnout of voters indicating Male/Female and their percentage in Lok Sabha Election

Year	*Turnout of Voters*			*Percentage of Voters Turnout*		
	Male	*Female*	*Total*	*Male*	*Female*	*Total*
1998	(Not available)	–	87,16,340	–	–	–
1999	(Not available)	–	10,18,2784	–	–	–
2004	56,953,52	46,77,812	10,37,31	72.82	65.03	69.09

Source: Election Branch, Office of the Deputy Commissioner, Nagaon, Assam.

Table 2.4

Growth Rate of Women Electors in Assam

Year of Election Held	*No. of Women Candidate*
1952	17,79,831
1956	(Not Available)
1961	22,21,900
1966	(Not Available)
1970	(Not Available)
1971	29,02,369
1977	36,69,027
1979	40,59,560
1985	45,80,946
1991	55,20,922
1996	57,30,170
2001	(Not Available)
2006	84,38,407

Source: Report on General Elections, 1952-2006.

Political participation of women at the grass root level institutions has been comparatively increased since the 73rd Amendment Act, 1993 and Assam Panchayati Raj Act, 1994 providing for women 30 per cent reservation of seat in PRIs in Assam. Total number of women representatives has reached the mark of more than 38 per cent after the last Panchayat Election in Assam in 2001 and in all three tiers of PRIs in Assam and has been found touching the mark of 33 per cent, (Sarma, 2006.)

Table 2.5

Election 2001 of Elected Members of Z.P., A.P. and G.P. District-wise, Male and Female

Name of District	*Z.P.*		*A.P.*		*G.P.*	
	Male	*Female*	*Male*	*Female*	*Male*	*Female*
Karimganj	13	7	65	31	720	336
Hailakandi	8	3	39	23	459	218
Cachar	18	9	102	60	1164	629
Dhubri	10	9	95	55	1086	564
Goalpara	11	5	51	30	574	291
Bongaigaon	5	1	39	16	356	248
Kamrup	18	11	102	57	1110	618
Nalbari	8	4	41	21	448	210
Barpeta	17	8	81	40	817	492
Darrang	5	3	39	22	404	267
Santipur	22	10	98	60	967	745
Nagaon	27	14	145	93	1619	1005
Marigaon	8	5	50	35	551	372
Jorhat	14	9	69	41	692	519
Golaghat	11	6	62	39	664	443
Sivasagar	16	8	75	43	748	549
Lakhimpur	11	6	53	28	601	289
Dhemaji	5	2	40	25	379	319
Dibrugarh	14	9	56	36	544	467
Tinsukia	14	6	53	35	584	370
Kokrajhar	0	0	2	1	21	12

Source: Rejuvenating Panchayati Raj Ideology Indian State and Lessons Periphery, pp. 234, 235.

Table 2.6

Elected Anchalik Panchayat Members and seats Reserved for SC, ST. and Women

Name of District	*Elected Women Member*			*Of Total Elected Member*
	Gen.	*SC*	*ST*	
Karimganj	24	4	–	96
Hailakandi	16	3	–	62
Cachar	43	10	1	162
Dhubri	52	5	6	150
Goalpara	22	–	3	81
Bongaigaon	16	3	–	55
Kamrup	46	4	4	159
Nalbari	19	1	–	62
Barpeta	21	5	–	121
Darrang	14	1	2	61
Santipur	35	8	7	158
Nagaon	58	17	8	238
Marigaon	20	5	3	85
Jorhat	30	3	3	110
Golaghat	25	4	6	101
Sivasagar	31	3	2	118
Lakhimpur	18	–	4	81
Dhemaji	11	1	5	65
Dibrugarh	29	1	3	92
Tinsukia	28	1	1	88
Kokrajhar	1	–	–	3
Grand Total	**559**	**79**	**58**	**2148**

Source: Rejuvenating Panchayati Raj, Ideology and Indian State and Lessons from Periphery: Bhupen Sarma pp. 236, 237).

Table 2.7

Elected Anchalik Panchayat Members and seats Reserved for SC, ST. and Women

Name of District	Elected Women Member			Of Total Elected Member
	Gen.	SC	ST	
Karimganj	252	34	–	960
Hailakandi	172	20	–	615
Cachar	440	71	7	1630
Dhubri	560	37	–	1500
Goalpara	92	–	32	784
Bongaigaon	173	39	8	549
Kamrup	409	30	40	1569
Nalbari	179	4	5	596
Barpeta	335	29	8	1188
Darrang	218	19	2	610
Santipur	407	41	38	1554
Nagaon	741	106	47	2384
Marigaon	217	58	54	838
Jorhat	364	16	7	1100
Golaghat	302	30	36	1006
Sivasagar	425	16	18	1179
Lakhimpur	169	12	51	809
Dhemaji	105	1	73	633
Dibrugarh	305	15	52	918
Tinsukia	286	11	25	866
Kokrajhar	9	–	–	30
Grand Total	**6160**	**590**	**530**	**21318**

Source: Rejuvenating Panchayati Raj, Ideology and Indian State of Lessons From Periphery: pp. 238, 239.

Table 2.8

Elected Zila Parishad Members and seats Reserved for SC,ST and Women

Name of District	*Elected Women Member*			*Of Total Elected Member*
	Gen.	*SC*	*ST*	
Karimganj	6	1	–	20
Hailakandi	3	–	–	11
Cachar	7	2	–	27
Dhubri	7	1	–	19
Goalpara	4	–	1	16
Bongaigaon	1	–	–	6
Kamrup	9	1	1	29
Nalbari	4	–	–	12
Barpeta	7	1	–	25
Darrang	3	–	–	8
Santipur	9	2	-	32
Nagaon	8	2	1	41
Marigaon	3	1	1	13
Jorhat	–	–	–	23
Golaghat	4	1	1	17
Sivasagar	6	1	–	24
Lakhimpur	4	–	1	17
Dhemaji	1	–	1	7
Dibrugarh	6	1	1	23
Tinsukia	2	3	–	20
Kokrajhar	–	–	–	–
Grand Total	**94**	**17**	**8**	**390**

Source: Rejuvenating Panchayati Raj, Ideology and Indian State of Lessons From Periphery: pp. 240, 241.

Table 2.5, 2.6, 2.7, 2.8, reflecting an ascending trend of women participation in PRIs more precisely from the last election, 2001 in Assam. But in some areas more especially in the district of

Kokrajhar elected woman members in all levels is extremely low. Women of those areas lacking awareness of their political rights resulting in having less interest in active political affairs. Large scale mobilization by conscious personalities and agencies both governmental and non-governmental in such localities is urgently needed for their socio-economic-cultural upliftment and political awareness.

Discussion

The participation of citizens in the political process in any nation associated closely with the availability of political rights. In India such rights are well mentioned and provided by the constitution equally to both men and women. But even after 57 years of working of the constitution women are yet to fully realise their different constitutional and legal rights to enjoy social, economic or political liberty. This is one of the main reasons for low percentage of women involvement in active politics. Thus, their participation in politics is yet to get momentum both in the national political forum as well as in the polity of Assam.

In case of tribal societies of Assam almost 90 per cent of women are involved in household affairs as workers in agricultural fields, weavers, collecting firewoods, fishing. They are socially more free than their counterparts in plains. Prejudices like Purda, dowry systems, and impediment on widow remarriage are completely absent in their societies. But most of them are illiterate and absolutely Greek of their important part in the national building process. But from last decade tribal women also have come forward and actively participating both in formal and informal political matters in the state. We could see a number of Cabinet Ministers bedecked the state Legislative Assembly of Assam like Srimati Pramila Rani Brahma, (Cong.), present Agriculture Minister, Srimati Rekha Rani Das Boro (AGP). Women from tea community yet to represent in the state politics.

Factors for astoundingly low figure for women participation in political process in Assam in particular and in the nation in general are mainly for traditional socio-religious cultural ethos of the society when women are considered as the 'passive', home-oriented', subordinate ingredients and an affair predominantly related to male counterpart only. The fabulous mind-set generated in the middle age is still lingering on even in this age of digital techniques and scientific fire of ours. But it is also true to note that due to lack of interest and self-security they are mostly reluctant to join in politics in Assam. A few women who have entered into active political life had either a long political background or from families with liberal outlook or they are educated. In the last General Election in 1991 the total number of contestants in the election for Lok Sabha seat in Assam, (14) was 166 and out of which only five were women, the percentage was only 3 per cent. Three of them were independents and the political parties one by Janata Dal and the other by Asom Jatiyatabadi Dal nominated two. Not any of the political parties offered party tickets to women in Assam election in 1991 (Women of Assam, Medhi and Dutta, pp78). In the last two elections held in Assam (2001, 2006) number of women contestants increased but a few could return winning in the fray.

Non-participant gesture towards politics is generally imbibed by women again from the socio-traditional norms prevailed in the society because right from their childhood they are treated as discriminated unit when they have to face with a thousand 'no', 'do not', 'should not' specially meant for them. They judge themselves inferior and their sentiment of feminist prefer to confine to household affairs, bearing and rearing children. It is also for their backward attitude towards their life as social, political men deferred them from entering into political life with conscious and matured political behaviour. Generally women feel shy to participate in debates, discussions barring a few as former Prime Minister Mrs. Indira Gandhi, Srimati Sushma Swaraj and a few more in the national level and Pushpalata Das, Srimati Vijoya Chakravarty from Assam.

Social structural constrains also add to adverse affect on the life of women and preferably like to manage household chores from their childhood. In the latter period also they find it extremely unusual and difficult to shun the sentiment habitual and groomed with. They have to rely upon their male counterpart even for a very trifling matter and fail to take part in the process of decision making in the social, faminial or political matters. Many a time it is also seen that to cast their valuable votes in time of election their male counterparts guide them. Cultural application on the issue of political participation of women both in Assam and in India in the political process on the part of the political parties is absolutely necessary in order to develop political culture in the system itself. In time of election, declaration for political parties make 10-20 seats exclusively for women candidates but till today no party could stick to their electioneering messages concerning women issues. This can be termed as issue-based politics on the part of the political parties without concrete vision or mission to empower women politically. Delaying 33 per cent of reservation of seats for women both in the national and state level political platforms are suffice to uphold the contention in view. Women lacking confidence for such dilly-dally attitude on the part of the political parties as it is found on their part hesitant to provide party tickets to women which is what also seen in the political scenario in Assam.

In Assam only a few women could afford the expenditure incurred the electioneering process. This is also another hurdle hindering women participation in political life. The intellectual groups of women are mostly employees outside their native places while again minimise that opportunity for them to enter into active politics. Besides, most of them have to shoulder greater burden working in official and familial affairs and hardly have spare time to think over other matters. Frequent occurrence of violence, criminalisation of politics, restrain young girl child from going outdoor at night for security concerned ('Gabharu Chhayali' in Assamese) also some other major issues for keeping aloof from active political participation.

In the grass root institutions more than 80 per cent women representatives are from the background of maintaining household affairs and only 27 per cent of women in Assam having political affiliation (Sarma, 2006 pp. 211). In some of the rural areas women representatives in Assam, for instance, in Jorhat, Golaghat, Lakhimpur are rendering commendable services to the people for their 'common good' and many of them are highly desirable to contest for Assembly Election in future. It can also be termed as positive indicator when 64 per cent of women representatives in rural polity in Assam are encouraged by their family members and husbands to join in politics (Sarma, 2006 pp. 212). The PRIs are also the political platforms in rural areas in Assam to educate women themselves with proper political knowledge for political consciousness to part in the development process of the nation, the state and also their own self so much so in political life.

Ideologies of modernisation, globalisation have considerably changed the status of women also in Assam and a large number of girl child are now sent by their parents for better education or other occupational purposes even at their tender age which was rarely found a few years back in many parts of the state. They have found changed in their attitude towards their composite life but showing less interest in active political affairs for overgrowing corruption and malpractices on the part of the political leaders as nauseous patriots. An analysis shows that most of them like to either build their own career or to get married earlier for a secured and socially recognised life as they believe (Interviewed at least 20 girls from various parts of Nagaon Town, Assam).

Suggestions

For more participation of women in political life there must be awareness campaign organised by the political parties, NGOs and other eminent personalities of the state. Both the family and the community should encourage girl child to evolve to her full potentials as social, economic, political human beings.

All schemes concerning women both for formal and informal education up to the age of 14 years are to be vigorously executed to inculcate confidence in them through practical knowledge and information for better understanding of complexity of politico-social cultural aspects of the state for sustainable development. The amount of security deposit for nomination for women is to be reduced for their easier access to politics of the state. In order to make them positive in attitude towards their life and to take part efficiently in all spectrum of decision-making process they are to be efficiently trained by imparting educational training, organising seminars, fruitful discussions explaining their unique role in the nation building process. Economic liberty is the pre-requisite of all liberties to make a human being independent in all spheres of his/her life. Government and the other NGOs must take the full responsibility to materialise every project meant for economic empowerment of women.

Women are the best judges of their own agony. Therefore, to solve their sufferings as decision makers and as active participants in the process of legislation on issues concerning women their representation in large number is extremely felt. Traditional approach should be altered to more rational attitude towards women as gender inequality in the society is acquired and not inherited. It is a psychological proposition rather than anything naturally evolved. Thus, it can be modified by man for woman. Moreover, the posture of self-consciousness have to be altered into the stage of self-assessment to develop the sense of self confidence to overcome from the status of subservience. Women cells in all governmental departments are to be established to render justice to any injustice shown to any of them in working places.

Courses for schools, colleges and in universities special lessons are to be exclusively included concerning women's participation in freedom movement, reputed women officials, legislators, their importance as a unit of the nation building process, nominal rate of literacy and different measure to eradicate it, their work health, position in the social, familial spheres in order to make women to better understand and realise their respective standard, reverence.

Conclusion

The above analysis helps us to conclude that the general position of women in Assam has considerably improved. But they are still to occupy higher ranks in the state and in the local levels of polity in Assam when found only in 'soft' sectors, of political affairs as health, social welfare, handloom and textile though many of them had proved their capacity to shoulder their responsibilities efficiently. Efficient and eligible women should encourage to join in formal and informal political spheres by providing them with some special advantages such as reducing the age limit both in for national and state level politics, reducing the amount for electioneering process, to eradicate illiteracy, hunger, special involvement for women in political matters by providing political education both for nation and for the state, to provide them with various scopes to get them outdoor in conformity to the constitutional norm as they are declared as weaker section of the community. It necessitates making them understand of their political rights for more and more political participation in political life first as an individual then as a woman.

Let women of Assam along with India revive their lost glory, status, position of the ancient age, Vedic Age as 'Godess of Prosperity' ('Laxmi'), 'Goddess of Learning' ('Saraswati'), Godess of Sakti' ('Power')-(Durga, Kali). For this women have to make themselves versed in all arts including political aspects of life for better understanding of political life. Mahatma Gandhi said, "...... So long as women in India do not take equal part with men in all affairs of world and in religious and political matters we shall not see India's star rising". The same condition would be in the forefront of Assam too as said by Gandhi.

At fine, at present, it can be noted that women in Assam have made a great strides in all affairs of their life.

REFERENCES

Acharyya N.N., (1987), *A Brief History of Assam*, Omsons Publications, Delhi.

Barua D.P. and Kalita R., (1997), *Uchchatar Madhyamic Buranji*, Sri Saraju Printing Works, Hooghly.

Bhuimati A. and Kumar S.A., (2007), *Women in the Face of Globalisation*.

Bhuyan A., (2005), *Asamiya Mahila Paribartita Mulyabodh*, 'Priyo Sakhi,' an Assamese Monthly for Women.

Bhuyan S.K., (1965), Nabajiban Press, Calcutta.

Chandan P., (2005), *Political Dynamics of Women*, Akansha Publishing House, New Delhi.

Devi R., (1994), *Women of Assam*, Omsons Publication, New Delhi.

Gandhi A., (2006), *Women's Work Health and Empowerment*, Aakar Books Publisher, Delhi.

Kakati P.C., (2006), *Bina Asom Quiz*, Ajanta Printers, Kolkata.

Pilanithurai G. (ed.), (2004), *Dynamics of New Panchayati Raj System in India, Vol. IV, Empowering Women*, Concept Publishing Company, New Delhi.

Sarma B., (2006), *Rejuvenating Panchayati Raj: Ideology Indian States and Lessons From Periphery*, Akansha Publishing House, New Delhi.

Saikia P., (2007), *Nari Muktir Bisaye Yatkinchit*, 'Prantik,' An Assamese Fortnightly, Vol. XXVI, N. 20-16, September.

Singh J.P.(ed.), (1996), *The Indian Women: Myth and Reality*, Gyan Publishing House, New Delhi.

3

WOMEN IN POLITICS IN AN INDIAN STATE

Dr. DASARATHI BHUYAN*

Women politics is the least researched topics in our country. It is as neglected as the women are in the Indian society. For a long time the social scientists did not cast a serious look at the political behaviour of women. It was partly due to the backwardness of behavioural research in India. But the more important factor responsible for the dearth of women studies was the lack of due weight accorded to the women in the society. Even today women studies are very few in number and women politics as a field of research is still in its nascent stage. The present study is an effort to fill up this vacuum and contribute modestly to the pool on the political behaviour of women.

In this paper an effort will be made to find out the correlation between the social and economic condition of women , and their political behaviour. Secondly , it will try to find out if there has been taken place any marked change in the pattern women politics. It will be relevant to determine if the changes in their socio-economic status have led to corresponding changes in their political behaviour. Their political participation in the

* **Lecturer in Political Science, Bellaguntha Science College Dist. Ganjam, Orissa-761119, Ph. 09937452727**
Email: **dasarathi_bhuyan@yahoo.co.in**

pre-independence period and after 1947 would be studied. In order to determine the level of their political modernisation, their exposure to communication flow, level of political knowledge and awareness, the degree of their efficacy and legitimacy and political participation would be certain analysed. The attitude of women towards various social, economic and political issues would be examined.

Women politics is the most significant feature in Indian politics. The debate was at the center in the international arena in 1994 UN conference in Cairo, at UN's fourth international conference on women in Beijing in 1995, UN' social summit conference in Copenhagen in March, 1995. The United Nations international conference on population and development in1994 in its guiding principles states that "the human rights of women and girl child are an inalienable, integral and indivisible part of universal human rights. The full and equal participation of women in civil, cultural, economic, political and social life at the national, regional and international levels and the eradication of all forms of discrimination on grounds of sex are priority objectives of international community.

The Government of India has taken numerous measures and has honest endeavours to hoist the status of women and establish gender equality. The constitutional obligations as well as different plans, programmes and policies have laid emphasis on women empowerment. Article 15 of the constitution of India prohibits any discrimination on grounds of sex. Further, Article 15(3) clarifies that this provision will not prevent the state from making any special provision for women. Article 42 of the Constitution envisages that the state shall make provision for securing just and humane conditions of work and maternity relief. Besides, the Directive Principles of State Policy also urge that the state shall direct its policy towards securing adequate livelihood for women and ensuring equal pay for equal work for both men and women.

The dawn of Independence in India was expected to make women conscious and assertive and equal of men in all fields including politics. Politicisation of women had started with the freedom movement. However, the extent of their politicisation was not impressive. It was confined mostly to the elite structures of the society. It was hoped that with the dawn of freedom, women politicisation would penetrate all strata and sections of the society. They would not only cast their votes but also share power and participate in the policy making and policy implementation process.

Women constitutes half of the total population of Orissa. Orissa with an area of 1, 55,707 square kilometers has a population of 3, 16 59,736 persons, which constitutes 3.74 per cent of the population of India. Out of this, the male population is estimated at 1,60,64,149 and the female at 1,55,95,590 constituting 50.74 per cent and 49.26 per cent respectively. Of the total female population, 87.4 per cent resides in rural areas against 12.6 per cent only in urban areas. The Scheduled Caste female population of Orissa accounts for 22,67,285 in rural areas and 2,65,565 in urban areas, making a total of 25,32,853. Similarly, scheduled tribe female population is estimated at 33,45,064 in rural areas and 1,74,259 in urban areas, making a total of 35,19,323. Of the total female population 155,95,590, scheduled caste forms 16.24 per cent, scheduled tribe 22.57 per cent and others 61.19 per cent. (Orissa Review, July-1989, p. 15).

There was a big gap between men and women in Orissa in electoral field during the pre-independent era. This can be inferred from the fact that none of the three ministry of Orissa during the period, i.e., from 1936 to 1947 included any women. While Sarala Devi and Punya Prabha Devi were elected from the Cuttack town constituency, A. Laxmi Bai was elected from the Brahamapur constituency. Among the women legislatures Smt. A. Laxmi Bai was the Deputy Speaker of the Orissa Legislative Assembly from 29-05-1946 to 20- 02-1952 and Smt. Basant Manjari Devi was the Deputy Minister of Health in the Harekrishna Mahatab Ministry, who assumed the charge of office on 23rd April, 1946. (Orissa Reference Annual 2004).

After the Independence of India there had been a spectacular increasing in the political participation of women in Orissa. Many of them were contested in the elections to the Assembly and Lok Sabha. A few of them also appointed as the ministers both at the center and in the states. But except Basant Manjari Devi, others were not very influential. The real powers continued to lay with the male politicians. Although Basant Manjari Devi, the "queen mother Rajmata of Ranpur" was a prominent women political personality, but she lacked state wide influent. Up to the end of 1960's the political scene of Orissa was dominated by male leaders like Harekrishna Mahatab, Biju Patnaik, Rajendra Narayan Singh Deo, Nabakrishna Choudhary and Biren Mitra. Although Basant Manjari Devi had been the deputy minister she was, at best, a "decorative piece" of the cabinet of H.K. Mahatab and Nabakrishna Chaudhary from 1946 to 1959.

The mid-term election to the Orissa Assembly was held in 1961. A Congress party candidate Smt Saraswati Pradhan was elected from the Bhatali constituency in Sambalpur district. In June 1961, Biju Patnaik took over as the Chief Minister of Orissa. He accommodated to Smt. Saraswati Pradhan in his cabinet as a deputy minister of Education. In1963 a qualitative change took place in all India Congress organisation with many seniors laying down office under the Kamraj plan ostensibly to strengthen the party. Biju Patnaik, who had taken keen interest in the postulation and implementation of the Kamraj Plan, also stepped down from thc office in August, 1963. He was succeeded by Biren Mitra. (Orissa in turmoil, p. 123) She was inducted as a deputy minister of Education in the Biren Mitra's cabinet on 2nd October, 1963. But the students agitation thoroughly shook the foundation of Biren Mitra's government so much so that on February, 1965 he had to bow out of office. On February 21, 1965 Sadasiv Tripathy was sworn in as the Chief Minister. He again inducted Smt. Saraswti Pradhan in his ministry as a deputy minister of Education. Smt. Saraswati Pradhan served as a deputy minister in the Ministry of Biju Patnaik, Biren Mitra and Sadasiv Mishra from 1961 to 1967, the fact that she could not be promoted to the minister of state or cabinet rank.

The general elections in 1967 came off at the peak of anti Congress wave in the country. In line with many other states, the Congress suffered a debacle in the poll. The Swatantra –Jana Congress alliance having gained an absolute majority of 75 seats formed a coalition ministry with the Swatantra leader, R.N. Singh Deo as the Chief Minister. Jana Congress candidate, Smt. Anang Manjari Devi from Sukinda constituency, Smt. Swaraswati

Pradhan of the congress from Bhatli constituency and Smt. Ratna Prabha Devi a Swatantra candidate from Dhenkanal constituency were elected to the Orissa Assembly. In spite of, the formation of Swatantra—neither Jana Congress coalition Ministry, Ananga Manjari nor Ratna Prabha were included in the Ministry.

In the mid-term elections to the Orissa Assembly in1971 the Congress came out as the single largest party. Despite 12 women candidates contested none of them were elected to the Orissa Legislative Assembly. But a four party coalition government, was formed. The parties in the coalition government were Swatantra , Communist, Utkal Congress and Jharkhand. Sri Biswanath Das headed the coalition governmet as Chief Minister. Before the Mahatab who had suddenly replaced Binayak Acharya as the leader of Congress Legislative party, made a futile bid to form a Congress ministry with the support of Utkal Congress. He washed his hands off the move as soon as he felt sure that the Prime Minister did not want to have a government in the state under his leadership and Nandini Satpathy, who was very much active in the political scene and who particularly worked as the poll-manager in the state , was interested to use him as a tool to serve her political purpose in the state".

Contradiction and tension among the coalition partners over various issues on the one hand and bitter in fighting in the Congress over the party leadership on the other again vitiated the political life in the state. More than once the coalition ministry came to the brink of collapse because of intra-party dissension among the constituent. Some how, the coalition jogged on till June 1972 by which time ten members from the front under the leadership of the Swatantra minister, Gangadhar Pradhan, defefected to the Congress. The final blow came on June 19 ,1972 when the Utkal Congress decided to rejoin the Congress following a serious of secret dialogue, between the Utakal Congress leader Nilamani Routray and the Congress high command. In anticipation of such a situation the high command groomed Nadini Satpathy, then a Union Minister of state, for the Chief Minister's office long before the actual fall of the coalition. Accordingly Nandini Satpathy was sent from Delhi to Bhubaneswar to head the Congress legislative party which by that time had 94 members in the house of 140—a fantastic majority never enjoyed by any party in the Assembly. (Sunit Ghosh, p. 185)

The ministry was in reality a coalition of six factions each pulling in different direction. On 1st March 1973 when the Assembly was in session, the political situation took a sudden turn, 25 members of Congress party including two cabinet ministers defected from the Congress and joined the Pragati legislative party. In the morning of 1st March the Assembly was prorogued suddenly by an order of the Governor with immediate effect. Nandini Satpathy, tendered her resignation. (B.K. Patnaik, 130).

In the 1974 mid-term elections to Orissa Assembly the Congress emerged as the single majority party with 69 seats. Assured of the support of the CPI and the independence Nandini Satpathy formed her second ministry on March 6, 1974. The strength of Congress legislative party had subsequently gone up to 84 with the defection of 14 MLAs from the Lok dal (former Pragati Dal). For two years the ministry sailed smoothly—the emergency of 1975 having helped Nandini Satpathy to smother her detractors in the party. But serious intra party feud broke out over Satpathy's virtual non cooperation with the reconstituted state Youth Congress which enjoyed the patronagc of high command. The dissidents demanded for change of CLP leadership became strident as charges of corruption against the highest political authority in the state came out in a section of the press. Moreover Satpathy was accused of confronting the center and deviating from the national mainstream. Eventually she had to bow out of office on December 16, 1976. Mrs, Satpathy left the Congress party on 17 March 1977 and joined the newly formed Congress For Democracy (CFD). Later on she formed her own party Jagrat Orissa Party. But the party could not do much headway and she returned to the Congress in 1989 and became the president of the Orissa Pradesh Congress Committee.

Nadini Satpathy was succedded by Binayak Acharya. The Acharya Ministry was dismissed by the Morarji Desai government along with other Congress governments in nine states. The Janata Party led by Biju Patnaik swept the polls in the elections to the Assemly held on June, 1977. Nilamani Routray, took over the administration of the state on June 26, 1977. Neither the Acharya Ministry nor the Routray Ministry included a women minister.

Table 3.1

Number of Women Legislatures, (1952-2009)

Year	*Total Assembly Seats*	*Elected Women Candidates*
1952	140	03
1957	140	05
1961	140	02
1967	140	03
1971	140	00
1974	147	04
1977	147	06
1980	147	03
1985	147	07
1990	147	07
1995	147	08
2000	147	14
2004	147	11

Table 3.2

List of Women Legislators 1952-2008

1951-52 ELECTION

Name	*Name of Constituency*	*Party Affiliation*
1. Kumari Ramraj	Patamundai	Independent
2. Saraswati devi	Raj Nagar	Congress
3. Basant Manjari Devi	Ranapur	Congress

1957 ELECTION

Name	*Name of Constituency*	*Party Affiliation*
1. Anang Manjari Devi	Digapahandi	Congress
2. Jyotirmanjari Devi	Deogarh	Gana Parishad
3. Ratnaprabha Devi	Kishore Nagar	Gana Parishad
4. Basant Manjari Devi	Ranpur	Congress
5. KanaklataDevi	Badamba	Gana Parishad

(Contd...)

1961 ELECTION

Name	Name of Constituency	Party Affiliation
1. Saraswati Pradhan	Bhatli	Congress
2. Ratnaprabha Devi	Dhenkanal	Gana Parishad

1967 ELECTION

Name	Name of Constituency	Party Affiliation
1. Anang Manjari Devi	Sukinda	Jana Congress
2. Saraswti Pradhan	Bhatli	Congress
3. Ratna Prabha Devi	Dhenkanal	Swatantra

1971 ELECTION

Name	Name of Constituency	Party Affiliation
1.00	00	00

(Smt. Nandini Satpathy elected to the Assembly after becoming the Chief Minister)

1974 ELECTION

Name	Name of Constituency	Affiliation
1. Sudhansu Nalini Ray	Govindpur	Conress
2. V. Sugyani Kumari Deo	Khallikote	Utkal Conress
3. Nandini Satpathy	Dhenkanal	Congress
4. Sairindri Nayak	Jharsuguda	Congress

1977 ELECTION

Name	Name of Constituency	Party Affiliation
1. Rasmanjari Devi	Athagarh	Janat Party
2. Kiran Rekha Mahanty	Pipili	Janat Party
3. V.Sugyani Kumari Deo	Khallikote	Janat Party
4. Ratnamanjari Devi	Brahamapur	Independent
5. Nandini Satpathy	Dhenkanal	Janata Party
6. Sairindri Nayak	Jharsuguda	Congress

(Contd...)

1980 ELECTION

	Name	*Name of Constituency*	*Party Affiliation*
1.	Saraswati Hembram	Kuliana	Congress
2.	Chandrama Santa	Pottangi	Congress
3.	Nandini Satpathy	Dhenkanal	Congress (U)

1985 ELECTION

	Name	*Name of Constituency*	*Party Affiliation*
1.	Saraswati Hembram	Kuliana	Congress
2.	Umarani Patra	Bhogarai	Congress
3.	V.Sugyani Kumari Deo	Khallikote	Janta Party
4.	Chandrama Santa	Pottangi	Congress
5.	Parama Pujari	Umarkote	Congrss
6.	Nandini Satpathy	Dhenkanal	Independent
7.	Fidra Topno	Raghunath Palli	Congress

1990 ELECTION

	Name	*Name of Constituency*	*Party Affiliation*
1.	Kamala Das	Bhograi	Janata Dal
2.	Pramila Mallik	Binjharpur	Janata Dal
3.	Sushree Devi	Ali	Janata Dal
4.	Shanti Devi	Sorada	Janata Dal
5.	V. Sugyani Kumari Deo	Khallikote	Janata Party
6.	Usha Devi	Chikiti	Janata Dal
7.	Nandini Satpathy	Dhenkanal	Congress

1995 ELECTION

	Name	*Name of Constituency*	*Party Affiliation*
1.	Saraswati Hembram	Khunta	Congress
2.	Kamala Das	Bhograi	Janata Dal
3.	Usharani Panda	Aska	Congress
4.	V.Sugyani Kumari Deo	Khallikote	Janta Dal
5.	Parama Pujari	Umarkote	Congress
6.	Rosani Singh Deo	Kokasara	Janata Dal
7.	Nandini Satpathy	Gondia	Congress
8.	Bijayalaxmi Sahu	Cuttack	Congress

(Contd...)

2000 ELECTION

	Name	*Name of Constituency*	*Party Aiffliation*
1.	Draupadi Murmu	Rairangpur	B.J.P
2.	Kamala Das	Bhograi	Biju Janata Dal
3.	Pramila Mallik	Binjharpur	Biju Janata Dal
4.	Nibedita Pradhan	Cuttack (Sadar)	B.J.P
5.	Mandakini Behera	Nayagarh	B.J.P
6.	Bijaylaxmi Patnaik	Khandapara	Biju Janata Dal
7.	Usharani Panda	Surada	Congress
8.	V.Sugyani Kumari Deo	Khallikote	Biju Janat Dal
9.	Usha Devi	Chikiti	Biju Janata Dal
10.	Mamata Madhi	Chitrakonda	Congress
11.	Parama Pujari	Umarkote	Congress
12.	Rosni Singh Deo	Kokasara	Biju Janata Dal
13.	Bishnu Priya Behera	Phulbani	Biju Janata Dal
14.	Anjali Behera	Hindol	Biju Janata Dal

2004 ELECTION

	Name	*Name of Constituency*	*Party Affiliation*
1.	Draupadi Murmu	Rairangpur	B.J.P
2.	Pramila Giri	Baisinga	B.J.P
3.	Sanchita Mahanty	Korei	B.J.P
4.	Surama Padhy	Ranapur	B.J.P
5.	Pramila Mallik	Binjharpur	Biju Janata Dal
6.	Bijaylaxmi Patnaik	Khandapara	Independent
7.	V.Sugyani Kumari Deo	Khallikote	Biju Janat Dal
8.	Usha Devi	Chikiti	Biju Janata Dal
9.	Hemabati Gamango	Gunpur	Congress
10.	Ajayanti Pradhan	Udayagiri	Congress
11.	Anjali Behera	Hindol	Biju Janata Dal

Table 3.3

Women M.Ps (Lok Sabha) from Orissa

7th Lok Sabha 1980 Election

	Name	*Name of Constituency*	*Party Affiliation*
1.	Smt. Jayanti Patnaik	Cuttack	Congress

8th Lok Sabha 1984 Election

	Name	*Name of Constituency*	*Party Affiliation*
1.	Smt. Jayanti Patnaik	Cuttack	Congress

10th Lok Sabha 1991 Election

	Name	*Name of Constituency*	*Party Affiliation*
1.	Frida Topno	Sundargarh	Congress

11th Lok Sabha 1996 Election

	Name	*Name of Constituency*	*Party Affiliation*
1.	Susila Tiriya	Mayurbhanja	Congress
2.	Frida Topno	Sundargarh	Congress

12th Lok Sabha 1998 Election

	Name	*Name of Constituency*	*Party Affiliation*
1.	Smt. Jayanti Patnaik	Brahmapur	Congress
2.	Sangita Kumari Singhdeo	Balangir	B.J.P

13th Lok Sabha 1999 Election

	Name	*Name of Constituency*	*Party Affiliation*
1.	Kumudini Patnaik	Aska	Biju Janata Dal
2.	Sangita Kumari Singh Deo	Balangir	B.J.P

14th Lok Sabha 2004 Election

	Name	*Name of Constituency*	*Party Affiliation*
1.	Sangita Kumari Singh Deo	Balangir	B.J.P

Table 3.4

Women Members of Rajaya Sabha from Orissa 1952-2004

	Name	*Term*	*Date of Election*
1.	Sailabala Das	1952-54	31-3-1952
2.	Nandini Satpathy	1962-68	19-3-1962
3.	Nandini Satpathy	1968-71	28-3-1968
4.	Saraswti Pradhan	1972-78	31-3-1972
5.	Susila Tiriya	1996-92	21-6-1986
6.	Mira Das	1990-96	21-3-1990
7.	Illa Panda	1992-98	25-6-1992
8.	Pramila Bahidar	2002-08	27-3-2002
9.	Susree Devi	2002-08	27-03 2002

Table 3.5

Profile of Women Ministers in Orissa

1.	**A Laxmi Bai** , Honourable Deputy Speaker, 30 June 1944, 23rd April 1946.
2.	**Basant Manjari Devi,** Minister of Health (Deputy), 23rd April 1946, 22nd May, 1959.
3.	**Saraswati Prashan,** Minister of Education (Deputy), 2nd October 1963, 8th March, 1967.
4.	**Nandini Satpathy,** Chief Minister, 14th June, 1972, 29th December 1976.
5.	**Sraswati Hembram,** Minister of Child Development and Rural Reconstruction, (Deputy), 9th June, 1980, 9th March, 1985, 2nd July, 1986, 3rd March 1990 , February 1999-05 March 2000.
6.	**Miss Frida Topno,** Minister of Fisheries & Animal Husbandry, (Min. of State)10th March, 1985, 3rd March, 1990.
7.	**Parama Pujari** , Minister of Health (Deputy), 22nd July, 1986, 3rd March, 1990, February 1999, 5th March 2000.
8.	**Dr. Kamala Das,** Minister of Education, Primary, 24th July, 1990, 15th March 1995, Health & Family Welfare (Cabinet) 4th March 2000, 6th August 2002.
9.	**Smt. Bijayalaxmi Sahu,** Women and Child Development, 15th March 1995, 5th March 2000.
10.	**Smt. Usharani Panda,** Minister of Health & Family Welfare, February 1999, 05th March 2000.

(Contd...)

11.	**Smt. Draupadi Murmu**, Minister of State for Commerce, 5th March, 2000,16th May 2004.
12.	**Smt. Bishnupriya Behera**, Minister of State for Women & Child Development, 6th August 2002, 16th May, 2004.
13.	**Smt. Pramila Mallick**, Minister of Women & Child Development, (Cabinet), 16th May 2002.
14.	**Smt. Surama Padhy**, Minister of Cooperative, 16th May, 2004.

Elections to the Orissa Assembly were held on 31st May 1980. Three women members were elected to the Orissa Legislative Assembly (Table 3.1). Sri J.B Patnaik was sworn in as the Chief Minister of the state on 9th June 1980. He inducted Smt. Saraswati Hembram , as a Deputy Minister of Child Development and Rural Reconstruction. Smt. Hembram continued as a deputy minister till the end of the J. B. Patnaik's first tenure of Chief Minister. (Table 3.5)

The tragic death of Mrs. Indira Gandhi in 1984 just before the 1985 elections created a sympathy wave in favour of the Congress party. One remarkable feature of this Assembly election was that 7 women members were elected to the Orissa Assembly. Never before such large number of women candidates were elected to the House (Table 3.2). Miss Fida Topno was inducted as the minister of state for Fisheries and Animal Husbandry in the second ministry of J.B. Patniak in 1985. J.B.Patnaik reshuffled his ministry on 22nd July 1986. Smt. Parama Pujari and Smt Saraswti Hembram as Deputy Minister's. Smt Pujari retained the portfolio of Child Development and Rural Reconstruction while Smt Parama Pujari was given the portfolio of Harijan & Tribal Welfare. (Table 3.5)

Following the election debacle in the Parliamentary elections of November 1989, J.B Patnaik who frustrated the efforts of all his political rivals to remove him from office resigned on 1st December,1989. Mr. Hemananda Biswal, a former critic and political rival of J.B.Patnaik became the leader of the Congress Legislature Party and he took over as Orissa's Chief Minister on 5th December, 1989. At the time of formation of his council of ministers, he was very conscious about taking the women members. He included all the women ministers of J.B. Patnaik's cabinet. Thus, Smt. Parama Pujari, Smt Saraswati Hembram, and Miss Fida Topno retained their portfolios till the ministry of Hemanand Biswal resigned on 3rd March, 1990 (Table 3.5).

Janata Dal under the leadership of Biju Patnaik captured power in Orissa in the March, 1990 elections to the Orissa Assembly. He took oath of Office and secrecy as the fourteenth independent Chief Minister. Seven women members were elected to the Orissa Assembly. Except Smt. Nandini Satpathy, a Congress Candidate, all others were elected from Janata Dal of Biju Patnaik. He inducted Dr. Kamala Das into his Cabinet as a minister of state for Education and youth services (Primary and Adult Education) (Table 3.5).

Elections to the Orissa Assembly were held on March, 1995. J.B. Patnaik himself was not a candidate in this election. All of a sudden he appeared as a father figure from the oblivion to head the Congress legislature party. Eight women members were elected to the assembly (Table 3.2). Among them Smt. Nandini Satpathy, Parama Pujari, Usha Rani Panda ,Bijayalaxmi Sahu, and Saraswati Hembram, were the prominent and high-flying members having previous political experiences . The job of selecting the cabinet and giving the portfolios was a neck-breaking exercise, and J.B.Patnaik was able to successfully accomplish this task in a cleaner manner. All the women members had an eye on key portfolios in his cabinet. During this time he made all of them impatient and restive. But at last dashing the high hopes of all the women members he inducted only one women member, Smt. Bijayalaxmi Sahoo, in his cabinet, and was given the portfolio of Women and Child Development (Table 3.5). This irked the other senior women members of the Congress Party in the Assembly. On August 26, 1998, J.B. Patnaik affected a mini cabinet expansion with reshuffling of portfolios of a few ministers. But he did not take any other women minister. The political scenario of Orissa gradually became worse with the Anjana Mishra molestation case. At the behest of political intricacies on 9th February, 1999 J.B.Patnaik resigned from his office. J.B.Patnaik was succeeded by Giridhar Gamango, a Member of Parliament from Koraput reserved Constituency. He inducted Usha Rani Panda, Parama Pujari and Swaraswti Hembram and Bijaya Laxmi Sahoo in his cabinet on February, 1999 (Table 3.5). In October 1999 it was the killer cyclone that devastated the state, leaving in its trail, death and destruction on an unprecedented scale. And then it was in the grip of a worsening political crisis no less debilitating in its effect. (Bhuyan Dasarathi , Janakiballav: A Political Biography, p. 108.)

As an internecine feud broke out within the ruling Congress over the leadership issue. Even Sonia, who handicapped Gamango in February to replace the unpopular J.B.Patnaik, had little sympathy for the man who was acknowledged as the most ineffective Chief Minister in the state's history.

For Gamango, house keeping was not that easy a job because of growing tension in the Congress Party for which the go-man-go himself was mainly responsible. As an administrator Gamango was not a great success. No significant headway was made in the relief operations in cyclone affected areas. Inherent contradictions and tensions among the Congress leaders over the party leadership that again vitiated the political life in the state. The succession to Gamango was not a problem. He was succeeded by Hemananda Biswal. He also retained all the women ministers of the Gomango Ministry without leaving any one of them.

The general election in 2000 came off at the peak of anti-Congress wave in the state. In Orissa the image of the Congress was smeared by corruption charges against the Chief Ministers of Congress. The Congress was practically routed in the Lok Sabha Poll just before the Assembly election in1989. Almost similar was the outcome of the Assembly election. The victory of Naveen Patnaik was never in doubt. He assumed the charges of office of the BJD-BJP coalition government on 5th March, 2000. Fourteen women members were elected to the Assembly for the first time (Table 3.2). This was the highest number of women members ever elected to the Assembly. It was only in 2000 elections that there were some changes in the political balance between men and women. He inducted Dr. Kamala Das into his Ministry as the Cabinet Minister of Health, Family Welfare, Women & Child Development. The Naveen Patnaik Ministry also gave berth to Smt. Draupadi Murmu as a Minister of State for Commerce and Transport. But in 2002 he dismissed Dr. Kamala Das from his Ministry on the charges of corruption and after the reshuffle of the Ministry on 6th August 2002 he included Bishnupriya Behera in his Ministry as the minister of state for Women and Child Development. He also suspended Smt. Kumudini Patnaik, Member of Parliament from Aska constituency, on April, 2002 to avert a possible split in the Parliamentary party. In order to prevent a formal split in the Parliamentary Party , Bishnu Priya Behera, wife of party M.P. Padmanav Behera were accommodated in the ministry. The suspension of Kumudini Patnaik assumed significant, as she was the wife of senior B.J.D leader and former finance minister, Ramkrishna Patnaik. Angry with the Chief Ministers' decision to sift him to agriculture minister, Ramakrishna Patnaik had resigned from the BJD-BJP ministry. In a mark of revolt the Patnaik couple resigned from the B J D and joined the opposition Congress Party.

The clean image of Chief Minister Naveen Patnaik working in tandem with the Vajpayee factor, won another term for the Biju Janata Dal — Bharatiya Janata Party alliance. Yet the 2004 Assembly Election was the toughest battle for the BJD-BJP alliance. Naveen assumed the office of the Chief Minister for the second time on May 16, 2004. The new Assembly elected 11 women members and among them were very few strong women leaders (Table 3.2). He inducted Smt. Pramila Mallik, as the Cabinet Minister of Women & Child Development and Smt. Surama Padhy, as the Minister of State for Cooperation. Naveen Patnaik sought to protect the "clean image" of his government by asking Women and Child Development Minister Pramila Mallik, who had a non bailable arrest warrant pending against her, to resign from the State Cabinet. By this move, he seemed to take some of the sting out the Opposition parties, which were preparing to raise the issue of tainted Ministers in the Assembly on July 26, 2004 following media reports that a warrant was pending against Mallik since 2003. But the very next day another media report brought to light a similar warrant pending against Higher Education Minister Samir Day, providing the Opposition led by the Congress fresh ammunition to mount pressure on Patnaik to act. The Opposition demanded that Day quit his ministerial post like Mallik. The high drama over the pending warrants against Mallik and Dey brought to the fore several issues concerning politicians with criminal backgrounds as also the fissures in the ruling Biju Janata Dal — Bharatiya Janata Party alliance.

The warrant against Mallik, who was heading the BJD's woman's wing, pertained to a case in which she allegedly led a mob that attacked Block development Officer, Siddharth Dhal at his office in Binjharpur, Jajpur district, in January 1999. The one against Dey was issued in a case relating to his participation in a roadblock agitation in 1995. The court of the Sub-divisional Judicial Magistrate of Jajpur had issued the warrant against Mallik three times. But it was not executed until the media reported its pending. The former Officer-in-charge of Binjharpur police station, B.K. Jena, was suspended on the charge of suppressing the arrest warrant. But unlike Naveen Patnaik, who sacrificed Mallik to protect his "clean image", the BJP stood firmly behind Dey maintaining that the case against him was not a serious one and that there was no question of his quitting the Cabinet. Later on Pramila Mallik was reinstated in the cabinet of Naveen Patnaik . (Bhuyan Dasarathi, Naveen Patnaik: the Best Chief Minister, 2006, p. 93).

The above analysis of the women participation in the administration of the state suggest that the women legislators elected so far mostly belong to the elite and high castes groups. The Khatriyas (rulers of ex-princely states) have contributed the largest number of women legislators. The noticeable supremacy of Khayatriya women over other women in the field of politics is mainly due to the feudal ruling backdrop and influential temperament. Before independence there were 26 Garajats or princely states whose rulers were designated as kings enjoying substantial fidelity to their subjects. Besides, there were a large number of Zamidars who were also in the surrounding area known as kings and wielded parallel authority over their subjects. Most of the princely rulers had thought that they would be rejected by the subjects after the independence. For that reason they opposed the freedom movement as well as the merger of princely states. But, contrary to their expectation, they did a good job in politics. It is imperative to note that, up to 1971 not a single Brahmin woman could be elected as an MLA despite the fact that it as one of the "Dominant Castes" of the state. It was after only in 1972 the Brahmins, Karans and Khandayats entered into politics. The representation of Oriya women in the Parliament election is very miserable. It is pertinent to note that till 1980 not a single women from Orissa was elected to the Lok Sabha. It was only 1980 Smt.

Jayanti Patnaik, wife of former Chief Minister, J.B. Patnaik was elected to the Lok Sabha. (Table 3.4). Since1980 only ten women so far have been elected to the Lok Sabha and since 1952 ten women have been elected to the Rajya Sabha. (Table 3.3).

Orissa is one of the poorest states in India with a semi feudal economy and a predominantly conservative culture. All the way throughout our history the men have taken the central stage. The men have typically subjugated the management and authority structures.

The emergence of the Oriya women in the struggle for India's freedom is a thrilling episode. Their burning nationalism, supreme, valour and gifted organizational abilities are printed in the chronicles of Indian Freedom Movement.

The political activities of the Oriya women reached its climax during the period of the Quit India Movement. A large number of women in Orissa contributed to the Freedom movement. Prominent among them are Rama Devi, Sarala Devi, Malati Chodhary, Arnapurna Maharana, Subhadra Mahatab, etc. After India became independent there was some increase in the political participation of women. Some women contested in local and general elections. Few of them were appointed as Minister both in states and centre. But the real power rested with man. It is true that Mrs. Gandhi played a long period as the Prime Minister of India. Her coming out as the Prime Minister of India was largely due to the fact that she was the daughter of Jawaharlal Nehru, the most important political leader of free India. Thus, the political ascendancy of Mrs. Gandhi does not really signify any general improvement in the political status of Indian women.

In Orissa a small number of women have become ministers. But they were not very influential. Still today male leaders are the dominated traits in the political scene of Orissa. In 1971 Mrs. Nandini Satpathy became the first women Chief Minister of Orissa. She sustained as the Minister of Orissa up to 1976. In spite of an effective administrator and strong politician, Mrs. Satapathy was forced to resign in 1976. Although she dominated the political scene of Orissa for five years, her political supremacy did not signify any significant women power in Orissa politics.

Due to their poverty, illiteracy and conservatism women are hardly discussing politics. They only discuss social matters and social issues. As well the women are very meager in respect of reading newspapers and listening to radio or on news bulletin on television. Only very small number of them discusses politics or read about politics. In addition to this, the conservative culture of Orissa greatly discourages to join politics; it is social taboo for them. By and large the people disrespect any women moving freely with men in political organisations and forums. Therefore, in the political socialization as well as in the political recruitment Orissa women are very trivial.

It is appealing to observe that political participation and political requirement in Orissa is confined to the higher status women class only. Some female members belonging to higher castes like Brahmin, Karan and Kshyatriyas have been elected to political posts both to the Panchayats and to the assembly and to the parliament. But in recent past due to the introduction of reservation in representation, some scheduled caste women and scheduled tribe women are getting involved in politics. Some of them are elected MLAs and MPs as a result of the reservation policy of the government. It is important to note that the election success of scheduled caste or scheduled tribe women is merely symbolic. They are just "token elites" without exercising any power.

A huge numeral of women goes to the polling booths in order to cast their votes. In terms of voting, their record in political participation is impressive. They did not give their vote according their option. They just vote as advised and instructed by her husband or another important member of the society.

There are hardly any cases where the wife differs from her husband in regard to their electoral selection. The women are scarcely seen vigorous in organising party meetings and political processions. They do not go there on their own choice. They are prejudiced by the male members of particular families to be present at political meetings or take part in political procession. This depicts that the political participation of women is very insignificant in Orissa.

Political empowerment of women is the determining factor for development and nation building. Our development has become lopsided due to denial of opportunities to women to participate in the many spheres of life. "As long as women of India," declared Mahatma Gandhi in 1925, "do not take part in public life there can be no salvation of the country," He further added, "as long as .... women do not come to public life and purify it...we are not likely to attain Swaraj." Even if we did," he added, "It would have no use for that kind of Swaraj to which such women have not made their full contribution."

We are yet to realise the vision of Mahatma Gandhi. It is said that, "doors to economic and political opportunities for women have been opening more slowly reluctantly and" "the continuing exclusion of women from many economic and political opportunities is a continuing indictment of modern progress. " Today women are in the forefront to put an end to this sad chapter of human history.

Women getting the right to vote in America have been considered as more important than manufacture of atom bomb, establishment of United Nations and many other great scientific discoveries. We can say with great confidence that if such is the importance of women getting rights to vote then their full participation in political and economic field will become the most far reaching the important event in the history of mankind. (Narayanan Usha, Economic and Political Empowerment of Women, Orissa Review, p, 57.)

We know from our experience that empowerment women through reservation of 33 per cent of seats for them in the Panchayati Raj Institutions have inducted almost one million women to public life at the grass root level. It has empowered the marginalised women and brought about significant social changes. The drive for literacy and antiliquor movements in many parts of the country has got an impetus from women's participation in Panchayat Raj bodies. Such political empower has encouraged women to move from one village to another to spread literacy with a catchy slogan ' Jai Akshar" which they say is equal in importance to 'Jai Hind' . Women are now restless to widen their public participation. It is evident from the answer of some rural ladies in Haryana who when asked about the meaning of good life said "women's participation in decision making ".

Adoption of women's reservation bill which aims at ensuring 33 per cent reservation in Parliament and state Legislatures will bring about a revolution in our country. It will in fact fulfill one of the dreams of Mahatma Gandhi who had gone to the extent of saying in 1946 that women should be preferred to men even if such preference resulted in total displacement of men by women.

Women's participation in the decision making bodies has the potential to cleanse the political process of criminalisation and corruption and ensure peace. There is prevailing opinion that the increasing trend of malpractices and violence deter women from coming to public life. But the revers is also true. Women's participation will lead to the improvement of standards of public life. As early as 1929 Mahatma Gandhi had prophetically written that "women is the embodiment of sacrifice and suffering, and her advent to public life should therefore result in purifying it , in restraining unbridled ambition and accumulation of property." Incidences of rape, molestation, dowry killing, female infanticide and domestic violence against women are increasing in alarming proportions. This is the result of inferiority status of women in society. We can reverse this by Politically Empowering women.

REFERENCES

1. Bhuyan Dasarathi, Naveen Patnaik: *The Best Chief Minister*, Indian Publishers Distributors, Kamala Nagar, Delhi, 2006, p. 93.
2. Panigrahy. R.L & Bhuyan Dasarathi , *Women Empowerment*, Discovery Publishing House, New Delhi, 2006.
3. Orissa Reference Annual-2004, Information and Public Relations, Govt. of Orissa, p, 325-381.
4. Narayanan Usha, *Economic and Political Empowerment of Women*, Orissa Review, January, 2002, p. 57.
5. F.G. Bailey, *Parliamentary Government in Orissa, 1947-1959*, Journal of Commonwealth Studies, (London) Vol. 1, 1961-1963, pp. 112-122.
6. N. Hazarika, *Role of Women in State Politics (Assam)*, Indian Journal of Political Science, Vol. 39, No. 1, January-March, 1978. pp. 61-78.

7. Ghosh Sunit, *Orissa in Turmoil*, Book Land International, Bhubaneswar, 1979, p. 149, 153.
8. Patnaik Balkrishna, *Politics of Floor Crossing in Orissa*, Santosh Publications, Brahmapur, 1985.
9. *Women and Social Justice* by M.K. Gandhi, Navajivan Publishing House, New Delhi, 1947.
10. *The Role of Woman* by M.K. Gandhi, Bharatiya Vidya Bhavan, Bombay, 1964.
11. Baral J.K. and Jena B.B., *Orissa Government and Politics*.
12. Fadia B.L., *Indian Government and Politics*, Sahitya Bhawan, Agra 1996.
13. Gandhi M.K., *The Role of Women*, Bombay 1964, Bharatiya Vidya Bhavan.
14. Gupta Giri Raj, *Family and Social Change in Modern India*, Vikash, New Delhi, 1976.
15. Patnaik Sudhakar, *History of Freedom Movement in Orissa*, Cuttack – 1951, Vol. III.
16. Employment News Dt. 24-30 June 2000, *Political Empowerment of Women* by Rashmi Thakur. Politics in India, March 1999.
17. Economic and Political Weekly, July 31st, 1999, Vol. XXV, No. 31.
18. Economic and Political Weekly, Jan. 9th, 1999, Vol. XXIV, Nos. 1 & 2, dt. 28.09.75.
19. *Orissa Review*, Vol. IV, No. 7 & 8, Feb-March, 2000.
20. Bhuyan Dasarathi, *Janakiballav: A Political Biography*, Indian Publisher & Distributors, Delhi, 2006.
21. Nayak Ganeswar, *Women of Orissa on the Wane: A Population Profile*, Orissa Review, July, 1998, 15, p.
22. *Politics in India*, April 1998, Vol.II, No. 10.
23. *Who's Who in Lok Sabha* in 1952 to 1991.
24. *Who's Who in Rajya Sabha* in 1952 to 1991.
25. *Yojana*, Vol. 44, No. 2, Nov. 2000.

4

DEVELOPMENTS IN SOCIAL AND ECONOMIC STATUS OF WOMEN IN INDIA

A STUDY IN ORISSA

Dr. B. ESWAR RAO PATNAIK*
Miss. PRASANTI PATNAIK**

SECTION-1

Introduction

Women empowerment is a global issue, which has gained momentum is recent decade. Gender inequality is at once ideological (the beliefs, norms and values about the status and roles of women in society) and structural (women's access to and positions within social institutions). As highlighted by Bradely and Khor (1993) political status includes women's access to power and representation in the state. Social status includes, women's access to education health as well as their sexual objectification and reproductive rights (Md. Tarique and Ahmed Sultan, 2006). In economic status, we include women's activities around production, distribution and consumption of goods and services. Several developing countries present gender inequality in employment, education and health outcomes. Women and girls

* Reader in Economics, S.B.R. Women's College, Berhampur.

** C.E.T, III Year Textile Engineering, Bhubaneswar.

in south Asia and China are prone to high mortality rates which have been referred to as the missing women by Amartya Sen. As the UNDP Report, 1995, observes employment and pay differences by gender are typical features of developing regions.

The declared goals of UN as embodied in Millennium Development goals are to eradicate poverty and hunger, achieve universal access to Primary education, reduce child mortality, combat with some fatal diseases, ensure environmental sustainability and develop a global partnership for development and all these goals are linked with gender based strategy. The impact of liberalisation on women's job is not much pronounced because women are by and large unskilled and uneducated. Empowerment of women in its political, social and economic aspects had occupied the centre stage in the political economies of the world.

The Real Situation of Women in World

Boserup has argued that development is not gender neutral. Women are marginalised in the economy, as development gathers momentum because they gain less than men in their roles as farmers, traders and agricultural labourers (S. K. Mishra and P.K. Pandey, 2006).

Around the world the picture of women is as follows:

1. Of the world's 1.3 billion, poor about 70 per cent are women;
2. In the last century, only 24 women have been elected as heads of Government (Tapan Kumar Sandhilya and Bipin Kumar);
3. Women hold merely 10.5 per cent of seats in the parliament;
4. Of the one billion illiterate, two-thirds are women. HIV is common among women. Rural women produce more than 55 per cent of total food grown in developing countries.

There are estimates that suggest that the value of women's unpaid house work and community work is 35 per cent of GDP in the world.

India's Position

The Government of India has declared 2001 as women's Empowerment year. The purpose, was to create awareness of women's issues with active participation of men and women to initiate and accelerate action to improve access to and control of resources by women and create an enabling environment to enhance confidence self esteem and autonomy of women.

As "The Times of India" (7.9.07) editorially observes, the basic health indicators are grin. Life expectancy at birth, at 64 is more or less on a par with Bangladesh and Pakistan, while China and Sri Lanka can expect to live till they are 74. Infant mortality rate is 54 per 1000 live births against 23 and 19 in case of China and Sri Lanka respectively. India's maternal mortality rate at 301 per 100,000 live births is terrible, when compared to 92 in the case of Sri Lanka. The National Health Survey-3 tells us that, 46 per cent of young children are underweight, compared to 6 per cent in China and 31 per cent in Pakistan. Centre and state spending on health accounts for just 1.39 per cent of GDP or about Rs 57,000 Crore. Education gets a better deal with centre and state spending accounting for 2.87 per cent of Gross Domestic Product. An Indian can not be expected to be healthy after 54.

World Bank report on its health schemes in India identified projects worth 2 billion being corruption ridden. These programmes concern Malaria, Tuberculosis and reproductive and child health, three of the most critical areas in terms of the number of people affected or lives lost.

There is no reason why health should not be treated on par with education. Mid-day meals must be an integral part of Sarva Siksha Abhiyan. The central thrust of the Govert's health budget should focus on medicine, shortage of doctors and nurses, pre-natal and post-natal programmes as well as the nutritional needs of children below five years. As the World Bank points out mere funds alone will not do the trick. Private player must weigh in strongly in areas of hospitals and health insurance, so that access to health services improves. Just as poor health acts as a drag on productivity, a healthier population will spur growth even to more dizzy heights. The country is growing at 9 per cent in recent years.

Viewed against this backdrop, the present paper makes an attempt to discuss the extent of progress made by the State of Orissa in education, health and economic fronts in empowering women. The study is based on secondary data and primary data.

The study discusses plan exercises in Koraput district vis-a-vis Orissa province in women empowerment. The basis of the study is primary data collected from 389 households in Koraput region in 1987 by the Researcher on the basis of simple multistage Random sampling Technique.

Meaning of Empowerment

Empowerment is a multidimensional process that enables human beings to establish their full identity and acquire adequate powers in every situation of life. It provides greater access to knowledge and resources, greater autonomy in decision-making, greater ability to plan and organise one's life activities, and freedom from shackles imposed by customs, belief's and practices. What is true for any human being is equally true for women. (Dr. K. Vijayantimala and Prof. S.N. Ratha, 2007). The World Bank defines empowerment as the process of increasing the capacity of individual or groups to make choices and transform those choices into desired actions and outcome. Central to this process are actions which both build individual and collective assets and improve the efficiency and fairness of the organised context which government the use of these assets".

Women's Role in Society

In rural areas, women perform a major part of agricultural operations like breaking clods of earth, manuring, weeding, transplanting, harvesting and threshing. They are active partners in rearing of animals, and small-scale industries like, rope and basket making and handloom weaving. Thus, the burden shared by the women for the socio-economic development is two-fold, one on the domestic front and the other one on economic front. The difficulties of getting drinking water, fuel for cooking, and health stand as obstacles run their domestic front smoothly.

Discriminatory Thinking

In rural areas the activities performed by women are generally undervalued or not at all taken into account. The ideological assumption about women's position in the family that women as housewives must depend on husband's wages is used to define women's position, even when they do not have bread earning husbands. As Dr. Y. Yasodara observes (2007) the unpaid and invisible work loads at home are considered as non-economic activities as they do not come under the purview of market activity. Access to skilled jobs and education in loss income families are sex-specific. It is frequently the male child who continues with his education, while the female child drops out to substitute work for schooling. The National Sample Survey has computed one woman unit of work equal to two-thirds of that of a male worker. S.N. Tripathy succinctly remarks, that the percentage of women headed households in Orissa is 15 per cent.

Even in cases, where many of these workers are family bread earners, they are regarded as secondary workers, because they are regarded as housewives. Y. Yasadara observes succinctly that, the heavy firewood of 25 kgs load on their heads, working long distances to fetch water and for animal grazing affects pregnant women and elderly women with pre-and post natal hazards and backbone benching. 90 per cent Kendu leaf gatherers are women and children and finally the money will be snatched by men. The sex-role pattern is reinforced by parents, teachers and administrations and has caused differences in the behaviour of the two sexes.

SECTION-II

Educational Status of Women

Educational plays positive role in the eradication of poverty and unemployment. It enhances the knowledge and skill of workers, the chance to expand non-farm activities helps better understanding and rational use of farm resources and makes one confident to adopt new technology. The general level of literacy of the people of study areas was 29.21 per cent in 1987-88. The literacy level of females is awefully low i.e. 12.03 per cent. Planned economic development in the state of Orissa has increased the literacy status of Koraput region from 29.21 per cent in 87-88 to 36 per cent in 2001. The district has to catch up with the All Orissa literacy performance of 64 per cent in the ensuring years.

Plan endeavour in Orissa has embarked on the path of universalisation of primary education. Today, there is one primary school for every 3.7 kilometers area. The level of drop-outs at primary level is 43.6 per cent in 1998-99 and for the girl child the drop-out rate is 42.4 per cent. The convincing explanation for the undertaking tendency of drop-outs in school, are the prevailing high teacher pupil ratio (1:35), the phenomenon of one teacher in schools casual attendance of students, teacher's absenteeism, lack of study materials like maps, globes, books and playgrounds. In an effort to achieve universalisation of primary education, the Government of Orissa has introduced Mid-Day-Meals programmes in 41,604 primary schools in 1995. Efforts were made to encourage enrolment, attendance and retention of students in schools by provision of rice and dal to the tune of 745 calories per child in 6-11 years age group.

The statistics compiled by NCERT (2001) are worth noting. Today, 40 per cent of class rooms are without chalks and blackboards. Out of 42000 schools, 10000 schools are without houses. 55 per cent of schools have no facilities for drinking water. The posts of 40,000 primary school teachers are lying vacant. Literacy rate of females is 51.0 per cent. Backwardness of tribal population can be a growth depressing factor. The literacy status of S.C./S.T. population is 36.8 per cent and 22.3 per cent in Orissa (1991). In Koraput district S.T. literacy rate is 23 per cent and female literacy rate is 20 per cent.

Table 4.1

Poverty in Orissa

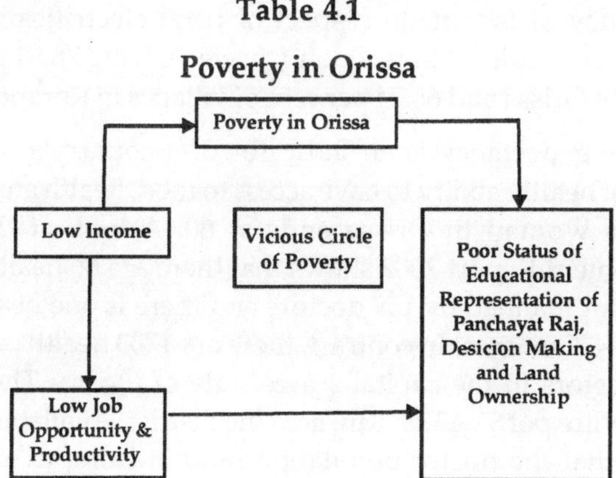

Arundhathy Chattapadhyaya, Yojana, June-2005

Barring 28 per cent of pucca houses, with tile or asbestos roofs, all other houses in the district are thatched ones, built mostly and owned by households themselves. Houses in villages were built mostly with locally available materials, like stones and bricks and lime for plastering. The 2001 census by Govt. of Orissa has focussed on availability of 2 rooms in the houses of people for maintaining the privacy of newly married couples. Sample households have 2 rooms only in 15 per cent cases in 2007 and latrine and drainage facilities were conspicuous by their absence in majority of houses. The low standard of living of people in Orissa and Koraput region is apparent from the fact that for sizeable population, Kerosene was the only source of fuel for lighting the house.

SOCIAL ECONOMIC CHARACTERISTICS OF THE REGION

Housing Conditions

Luckily enough, in study areas safe drinking water (by tubewell/hand pump) facility was available within the vicinity of residence of people in 60 per cent cases. In Orissa less than 45 per cent of people have access for safe drinking water near their residence.

So S.C. Chakravorty (1969) has observed that, the deplorable housing condition of majority of workers have contributed for the inefficiency of labour. In respect of rural electrification, rapid strides were made by the economy in electrifying 78.94 per cent of villages in Orissa and 66.74 per cent of villages in Koraput District.

Life expectancy is an indicator of a country's health and quality of health: ability to have access to food, health and services. Life of a woman in Orissa ends at 60. A look at the Orissa Development Report 2002 shows that there are 66 health Centres in Koraput manned by 159 doctors and there is one health centre per 133.44 K.m. area. In contrast, there are 1703 health centres and 21289 doctors in the capital scarce state of Orissa. There is one health centre per 91.43 sq. Km. area the district. Available statistics suggest that the doctor population ratio in Koraput and Orissa are 7061 and 7408 respectively.

The hospital bed ratio in Orissa is 1:2680. Planning efforts at state level have succeeded in providing one medical institution for 21,700 population. The state has made some headway in universalisation of vaccination to prevent the onslaught of diseases like, Polio, T.B., Diptheria, Tetanus and Woophing Cough. The per capita Governments expenditure on health and family welfare is Rs. 136.3 in 1999-2000.

The overall success of the Government in the task of ending poverty and ignorance and disease and inequality of opportunity has been limited. (B. Eswar Rao Patanaik 2005)

Health Conditions of Women

Poverty underlines the poor health status of women in Orissa. Reproductive health problems fall into the realm of "Private and unspoken "diseases" leading to a culture of silence. Most diseases go unreported. Majority of health professionals in rural areas are men and this adds to the hesitation of females to seek medical help. According to the second national family Health Survey, 1998-1999, only, 52 per cent of women in India are never consulted on decisions about their health. When children fall sick, boys are preferred to girls for seeking medical help. Poverty is the attributable factor for malnutrition of the girl child. Early marriage and pregnancies are disadvantages to them.

It seems that, the average Indian women is 100 times more likely to die of maternity related causes than a women in the industrialised countries. Analysis of maternal mortality in India shows that there are 407 maternal deaths per 100,000 live births, caused by hemorrhage, infection, obstructed labour, anaemia and abortion. Lack of proper care during pregnancy and child birth, deliveries at homes, lack of institutional deliveries and inadequacy of services of or vacancy position of 356 nurses and 136 doctors in Malkanagiri, Nobarangapur, Rayagada and Koraput districts reduce life expectancy at birth, of females, an important indictor of a country's level of health (S. S. P Shirna, Shiv Sankar and Yoginder P. Singh 2006).

Economic Empowerment of Women

As per 2001 census, the percentage of cultivators and agricultural labourers in Koraput district were 32.71 per cent and 40.24 per cent respectively. The proportion of other workers and workers in household industry in the region was recorded at 25.11 per cent and 1.94 per cent respectively. The percentage of cultivators and agricultural labourers in Orissa on the other hand was 29.75 per cent and 35.02 per cent in 2001. The work force structure of the district reveals a higher work participation rate of 48.46% in the district for above the state average of 39.38 per cent.

Earnings from agriculture are unable to maintain a tribal family in Koraput region for the whole year. They supplement their meager earnings through collection of minor forest produce, hunting, fishing, manufacturing of household art's and crafts materials, wage earning and service in private, public organised and unorganised sectors.

It seems that, the cropping pattern of the district is tilted in favour of paddy and cereals that claim 71.25 per cent of cropped area. Minor millets and commercial crops claim 14.46 per cent and 14 per cent of total cultivated land (1584.33 acres) respectively in study areas. The average size of land holding in Koraput district is 5.33 acres in 1987 and 2.5 acres in 2007. In sharp contrast, the average size of land holding in Orissa is 4.5 acres.

The average income of male cultivator per annum is Rs. 2345 as against the corresponding amount of Rs. 2338 for a female cultivator. The per acre yield of rice in Orissa is 7.59 quintals per hectare, while the yield rates are 35.64 qtls. per hectare, for wheat, 4.60 quintals, for Ragi, 2.28 quintals and for Mung in 2002-03. In the low income economy of Koraput, the per acre yield of paddy which was 12.8 quintals per acre in 1987 has stagnated at 11-0 quintals in 2007-08. The per acre yield of Ragi has shot up from 3.3 quintals in 1987 to 4.0 quintals in 2007-08. The cropping intensity is 141 in the backward district. In Orissa province, the percentage of net area irrigated to net area sown in 1990-2000 is 34.40 per cent (India-40.53%). Sub-division and fragmentation roughly covers 20 per cent of the cultivated area in the district. The scatteredness of land holdings preclude the possibilities of the use of improved agricultural practices, such as use of improved seeds, manures and pesticides. Disparities in land ownership may create unequal access to credit, other services, inputs and marketing opportunities (Sirish Patnaik, 1982).

It is well known that, appropriate farm implement's have played a key role in promoting optimum use of soil and water. As per the findings of D.A.O., officials Koraput, only 9.76 per cent of farmers (29 families) were using iron plough. Only 30 per cent of contact farmers were in possession of all the six agricultural implemented which were central for agricultural improvement namely: (1) Seed Drill (2) Iron plough (3) Puddler (4) Weeder (5) Sprayer and (6) Thresher. While the yield rate per paddy is 55 per cent higher for hybrid seeds, the farmers are reluctant to go in for package programme due its risk prone and costly nature and irritating delays in the supply of inputs by extension workers. Soil fertility is eroded due to excessive grazing felling, of trees, plough and Jhumming.

With regard to wages paid for agricultural labour, a male agricultural labourer used to receive Rs. 8/- for a day's work. While the average rate for Female agricultural labourer was Rs. 6/- per day. The Jeypore survey of 2007 by the scholar, has surfaced that there has been an upward revision in the wages of male worker from Rs. 8/- per day to Rs. 50/- per day and for the female agricultural labourer, there has been an upward revision in wages from Rs. 6/- per day in 1987 to Rs. 40/- per day in 2007. The workers were not paid wages at the officially declared rates by contractors. It follows that the lack of implementation of minimum wages Act and Equal Remuneration Act 1976 is a different on empowerment of women. The National Sample Survey has computed one woman unit of work equal to only one half unit of a male work.

In majority cases land records are tilted in favour of male persons. The wheels of agricultural progress of Koraput district are pushed backwards because, there is limited use of fertilisers (7.7 kgs. and 64 kgs. per hectare respectively in 1987 and 2007), the impact of tractors is limited to 4 households, and a priority input like irrigation claims 1.8 per cent of total outlay. In contrast 39.00 kgs. of fertiliser are applied per hectare of cultivated land in Orissa region.

In addition, the backwardness, of the district due to hill area backwardness, tribal backwardness, backwardness due to natural calamities and depletion of natural resources impede sanguine development of women workers of the region. Although, the district receives an average rainfall of 1521.8 mm, the actual rainfall recorded in 2000 in Koraput was 1359 mm.

The grinding poverty of women stems from the fact that agriculture is not a remunerative occupation. The gross income per acre of land, which was Rs. 1200 in 1987 was recokned at Rs. 3000 in 2007. Recent facts and developments in Koraput region suggest that, the peasants are unable to secure procurement price for paddy at the officially declared prices because F.C.I. do not purchase paddy from the growers directly. The women cultivators dispose of paddy to millers at unremunerative prices.

Political Empowerment of Women

Strengthening the number of women representatives in Panchayati Raj institutions is a sine-qua-non of successful planning at grass root levels. In the early decades, Indira Gandhi has accomplished Olympian success as the Prime Minister of India and Late Nandini Satapathy won laurels as the Chief Minister of the State of Orissa. An analysis of the following table 4.2 (*See on next page*) suggests that there were 85.3 women representatives in 197 Gram Panchayats of Koraput district in 2001. Only 26 women representatives have 04 urban local bodies.

Planning and Gender Development

Equality before law for women (Article 14)

1. The state not to discriminate against any citizen on ground of any religion race, caste, sex and place of birth (Article 15).
2. Equality of opportunity for all citizens in matters relating to employment.
3. The state has to secure for men and women equally the right to means of livelihood (Article 39) and equal pay for equal work.
4. The 73rd and 74th amendments to the constitution have incorporated 33 per cent reservation for women in local bodies.

Table 4.2

Category-wise number of Representatives in Gram Panchayats, Panchayat Samitis and local bodies of Koraput district (2001)

Category No.			General	OBC	S.C	S.T	Total	Men	Women
1.	GramPanchyat	197	771	–	369	1517	2657	1804	853
2.	Panchayat Samities	14	59	–	28	110	197	126	76
3.	Urban Local Bodies	4	51	–	12	14	77	51	26

Source: District Panchayat Office, Koraput.

5. Not less than one-third of the total number of officers of chairpersons in the Panchayats will be reserved for women (Article 243).

Tapan Kumar Sandilya (2006) refers to the following legislation's promulgated for protecting and developing women:

(i) Immoral traffic (Prevention) Act, 1956;

(ii) The maternity Benefit Act 1961;

(iii) The Dowry Prohibitions Act, 1961;

(iv) Indecent Representation of Women Act 1986.

(v) Protection of women from Domestic Violence Act, 1986.

The accent of the first five year plan (1951-1956) was on establishment of the central Social Welfare Board and organisation of Mahila Mandal. In the second Five year plan, the thrust was on intensive agricultural development women education has drawn the pointed attention of planners in the third plan with a thrust on service for maternal and child welfare, health, education, nutrition and family planning.

Family planning along with immunisation programme was the hall mark of the Fourth Five Year Plan. Supplementary feeding programmes, too have received due priority. The credit for setting up women's welfare and development bureau goes to Fifth Five Year plan which has highlighted on functional literacy and training women in need of income. The approach of the Sixth Five Year Plan (1980-1985) has witnessed a shift in focus from welfare to development. The Seventh Plan (1985-1990) has expressed concern for equity and empowerment of women by emphasising qualitative aspects such as inculcation of confidence, generation of awareness with regard to their women's rights and training skills.

The development oriented sixth and seventh plans have witnessed the birth of several social initiatives in favour of women. Some examples are Women's Development Corporations (WDCS), Support to Training and Employment Programmes (STEP), Awareness generation camps for rural and poor women, short stay homes for women and girls and women's training Centres for rehabilitation of women in distress.

Empowerment of women through Panchayati Raj institutions was envisaged in the Eight Plan. The pre-natal Diagnostic Technique Act, 1994, raises grave objection to immoral and unkind abortion of girl child in the womb of the mother. In the 9th plan, 30 per cent of out-lay was meant for women.

Conclusion

It seems fair to conclude, that the state of Orissa occupies a low area in the map of socio-economic development. There has been some headway in income levels, literacy and health status of people but these gains are moderate. The daunting task of planners of the state is to provide land and Patta's in women's names, prevent child marriage and polygamy recognise the interests of women, link more and more women to self-help groups, Micro-Finance programmes and Self-help schemes, strive for skill formation of women to facilitate income support, locate Primary Health Centres near their habitat and improve delivery mechanism. In education sphere, languages should be in their mother tongue in schools, syllabus should be in tune to their culture, teaching aids should be audio visual aids and incentives may be provided to tribal girls to study. As tribal girls can not go to school to look after siblings at home, childcare centers near the shelter of women may be provided. Lady teachers may be posted in schools. In employment schemes, efforts may be strengthened to generate 100 days of work per annum for a female worker in a year.

So, the scale of endeavour may be raised by public authorities, N.G.O.'s, People and Officials to wipe out tears from eyes of female's.

REFERENCES

1. 89th IEA Annual Conference Volume.
2. P.C. Mohapatro & B. Eswar Rao Patnaik, How Can We Improve the Socio-economic Conditions of Women" *Yojana*, May, 1988.
3. *District Statistical Hand Book*, Koraput 2001.
4. Dr. B. Eswar Rao Pattnaik *"Empowerment of Tribal Women in Orissa"*, Conference Papers, National Conference on "Empowerment of Dalit Women: Retrospect and Prospect", Ambdekar Centre for Research and Social Action, Hyderabad.

5. B. Eswar Rao Patnaik, *"Empowerment of Women Entrepreneurs in Koraput District"*, "Employment and Entrepreneurial Status of Women in Orissa" by K. C. Patra, Pattamundai College, Pattamundai Orissa.
6. B. Eswar Rao Patnaik *"Problems and Prospect of Agricultural Development in Koraput District* (Orissa) Unpublished Thesis.

5

STATUS OF WOMEN
A PROFILE

Dr. PRADEEP KUMAR SWAIN*
Dr. GIRISH DAS**

One of the most important changes that have taken place in recent time is the growing status of women, socio-economic advancement of a country can be rest judged by the status and position which it can bestow on its women. A nation would not march forward if the women are left behind. The leave of economic equality and independence are the real indicators to measure the status of women in any society. In India, the general economic situation is far from satisfactory, the situation of woman being worse than that of man. The female population constitutes nearly half of the total population in India. But now it is universally accepted that important development processes have bypassed woman at every stage.

A woman should get a proper status in the society. Her role should not be confined to routine household work but she should be made an important constituent of the society, which is called empowerment.[1] Today it is universally recognized that woman are integral to all priorities and development. World Bank

* Lecturer in Political Science, Boriguma College, Dist. Koraput, Orissa.
** Lecturer in Political Science, Kotpad College, Dist. Koraput, Orissa.

Development Report (1991) concludes that economic success for women will improve their own lives and those of all Indians. For the end, women's access to goods and services, to productive assets and to markets must be improved and brought probably at par with that of males.[2]

To improve the status of women and their role in the process of development, such development should be an integral part of global project for the establishment of a New International Economic Order based on equity, sovereign equality, interdependence, common interest and cooperation among all the nation states.[3]

A high level World Bank team put the gender related issues to the fore to ensure that the adverse impact of structural adjustment and stabilisation of economy did not fall on activities concerning women and child welfare, health, education and family welfare.[4]

Pandit Jawaharlal Nehru had rightly stated " the status of women indicates the character of a country.[5] In India, we started the team women's studies more frequently after the International Women's Year i.e. 1975, "Status may be analysed in terms of the extent to which a person is perceived to receive rewards incur cost as well as with the extent of his/her investment, his/her past history or background. (Secord and Backman, 1964 (p. 308)[6]

One of the ways to ensure gender equality is the empowerment of women. The strategy of the Government of India for the empowerment of women has been to reserve seats for women in education, in employment and most important of all in the Panchayati Raj institutions so that women are effectively able to participate in democratic decision making. There is no denying the fact that women in our days have begun to acquire the status of equality with men and several arena till recently closed to them. Nevertheless struggle for complete emancipation and equality goes on.[7]

Following are some of the indicators of women's status:

(i) Female infant mortality rate;

(ii) Maternal mortality;

(iii) Female literacy rate;

(iv) Women's age at marriage;

(v) Sex ratio;

(vi) Status of female child in the family and society;

(vii) Employment status of women;

(viii) Property rights of women;

(ix) Participation of women in political, economic and social life of the country;

(x) Incidence of social evils, such as sati, divorce, domestic accidents, rapes, dowry deaths etc.; and

(xi) Social and personal oppression of women. All the indicators put together would contribute the quality of life. It is said that the status of Kerala women is the highest in India, as she enjoys a better quality of life.[8]

In respect of status that is accorded to women by law and by the constitution, we notice that there is a gap between the theoretical possibilities and their actual realisation. It is true that scriptures and sacred texts provide scope for diverse interpretations and value emphasis at the hands of different authorities and at different period and of time. Religion has a dynamic character and is shaped and reshaped by historical processes and the interaction with the popular religion. Through different perods of history orthodox Hinduism has produced strong reactions and has resulted in he establishment of new religions of sects, such as Buddhism, Jainism, Sikhism, Veerasaivism and Vaishnavism and the 19th Century reform movements like the Brahmo Samaj and Arya Samaj.

In Hinduism, a women is described by a multitude of derogatory attributes. In Hinduism women is viewed on specific roles with the conception of marriages as the true destiny of a women and her important obligation to bear a son, the roles of wife and mother emerge as the proper roles for a woman.

The Bhakti Movement brought great solace to women and presented an alternative ways of life to many individual women. Men and women stand on a footing of equality in Islam. The two practices that have been most detrimental to the status of women in Islam have been talaq or unilateral divorce and seclusion of women. Christianity accepts equality between men and women in matters of religion. Buddhism elevated the status of women. Sikhism emphasises the householder's ideal and demands respect for women as men's helpmate and sharer in his domestic life. Zoroastrian women enjoy a position of honour in the family and the society.

From amongst the Western philosophers Plato believed in men-women equality through he did not concede this out of emotional reaction or humanitarian ground. Aristotle's approach to women is functional. He believes that all things derived this character from their function and they are thus due to their function they perform. Rousseau's views about women is the representative of the whole western world. He argues that women's sharply distinct position is due to those characteristics that are natural to her sex. Rousseau believes that, an average woman can manage very well by preserving her natural instincts at various levels of behaviour. In fact he gave out a long list of "feminine qualities" for women. Locke believed that familial authority belongs to the mother as much as to the father. Hobbe's attitude to women was a mixed one. According to Jeremy Bentham, that the sensibility of women is greater than men, they are inferior in physical strength and they are more sympathetic by nature. Mill aimed solely at the happiness of women through it was an important part of it. A great French philosopher and idealist Charles Fourier once said that one could judge the degree of civilisation of a country by the social and political position of women.

A global look, however, shows that with the social, educational, economic and scientific progress situation has undergone considerable change throughout the world. Today in any developed or educated society women in general are not taken and treated as a commercial commodity. There has been a lot of movements, agitations and legislations to improve the status and position of women.

Customs, traditions and social roles discriminate the women more severely than anything else. Because of such cultural ethos even large number of women oppose equal rights and privileges not only in under-developed societies but also in America (Frenier, 1984).

Although complete equal status of women and men is found nowhere, it varies from country to country and from society to society. In the light of the discussion made so far the following features emerge:

(a) That inequality in status of male and female is a global phenomenon. Women are adversely treated and are subjected to discrimination on ground of their sex;

(b) That the magnitude of discrimination and maltreatment to women, however varies in different countries and in different parts (or societies) of the same country;

(c) That there has been a global concern against the discrimination and maltreatment of women which has manifested itself in organised movements, agitations and adoption of legislations in many countries;

(d) That on account of growing concern, education, economic independence and measure adopted, the gap of inequality between two sexes has narrowed almost throughout the world[9].

The evolution of the status of women in India has been a continuous process of ups and downs throughout history. Considerably the vast body of empirical research available, two approaches seem to be valid. One is classical text view and the other empirical view.

Following are some of the strategies to raise the status of women in India: (1) Mass protest against dowry and social exploitation of women; (2) creation of mass consciousness about the status of women; (3) provision for training facilities of employment; (4) supportive services should be provided by the Central and State Governments and voluntary organisations for women in distress; (5) legal aid centers, mobile courts and counselling centers should be organised; (6) efforts should be made to organise the unorganised women work force to protect their rights and safeguard themselves from exploitation, insurance cover, maternity and other benefit should extended to unorganised women work force; (7) special cells should be created to enforce legislation of job security, working conditions, minimum wages, equal pay in equal work etc. which should be extended to the unorgansied sectors too; (8) different media should be involved to create awareness for women's education and their role in economic, social and political development of the nation, portrayal of women should properly done through media; (9) more productive beneficiary oriented schemes should be launched especially for women at the government and non-government organization; (10) more and more voluntary organisations should be encouraged to launch women development programmes; (11) ICDS programmes should be strengthened to ensure girl child equal access to health care, mother and child care and nutrition, vocational training, education, maternity and child welfare aspect must get interwoven with all the development schemes; (12) efforts should be made to remove sex bias and promotion of the value of equality through school curricula; (13) ban should be imposed on sex discrimination tests like amniocentresis, ultra scanning which led to medical termination of pregnancies; (14) the curricula in formal non-formal and adult education for women should include the areas like family education, health education, political and civic education, religions and moral education, vocational education; and (15) Political empowerment of women through reservation in Panchayati Raj Institutions vide 73rd Amendment should be effectively implemented.

On the whole, the government bodies in central, state and local level voluntary organisations and women's associations particularly Mahila Mandals at the grass root level and the media (both print and electronic media) and educational institutions both formal and non-formal should be created upto raise the status of women in India.[10]

Conferences and Committees on the Status of Women in India

While submitting the Report of the Committees on the status of women in India in 1974 to the Government the covering letter signed by its ten members reported that our investigations have revealed that large masses of women in this country have remained unaffected by the rights guaranteed to them by the Constitution and the laws enacted since independence. Our recommendations are made primarily with a view to making these rights more real and meaningful. We are confident that they will be considered in the light and measures for their implementation.

The Committees was constituted following a resolution of the Ministry of Education and Social Welfare an 22nd September, 1971 and the presentation of its Report coincided with the celebration of the International Women's Year in 1975. Contrary to what the Committee Report revealed there appeared the following year another comprehensive work by Tara Ali Baig—India's Women power though it was a personal study of the position of women. She does not completely agree with the committee's findings[11].

Since the First World Conference on Women, which was held in Mexico City in 1975 which has changed for the world's women, their education, salaries have increased, they have taken up high profile jobs and have become entitled of their own rights. At the same time however discrimination and exploitation has also increased and in many countries tradition and fundamentalism conspire to keep them as willful subordinates.

The year 1975 was declared as World Women's year. Later the decade from 1975 to 1985 was declared as Women's Decade. The International Women's Year (IWY) came as a boon for Indian women. The general aim of the I.W.Y. was to raise the status of women throughout the world. A U.N. message said that women from all countries and races should come out to strengthen their position in the society.

The Central Welfare Board conducted a number of state level seminars to study the real needs of women. The board brought out special numbers of its magazines. Social Welfare and Samaj Kalyan in connection with the International Women's Year. The main objectives of these seminars were to create an awareness among Indian women who had been suffering because of their ignorance. The National Plan of Action for Women (NPAW) stressed the need to educate women and the need for equality of opportunity.

Draft Platform of Action

The UN's Draft Platform of Action identifies "inequality in women's access to and participation in the definition of economic structures and policies and the productive process itself". One of its goal is the economic empowerment of women.

The Actions that the Draft Platform proposes to take are: (a) take positive actions to help women overcome barriers including targeting women to job programmes. Providing credit and introducing training in non-traditional areas of work, promote their access to technology, markets and trade; (b) promote equal pay for equal work; (c) create a supportive work environment, including parental leave and part, time work with benefits and flexible hours; (d) eliminate sexual harassment in the work place. It also lists twelve areas of concern, including education, health, violence, human rights, the environment, the girl child, political participation and the mass media. Two key points for discussion were economic deprivation of women and the feminisation of poverty.

The U.N. International Research and Training Institute (INSTRAW) has developed a framework for counting and valuing the unpaid and invisible economic contributions made by women. The U.N.D.P. has prepared two additional indices in 1995 for the first time, with the focus on the Beijing Conference. These are the Gender Related Development Index (GDI) and the Gender Empowerment Measure (GEM). In both these indices India scores very low showing the great disparity within the country.

WOMEN'S ASSOCIATION

National Organisation

The Women's India Association founded in May, 1917 did tremendous service to the cause of women. It was the first All India Organisation of Women to look at things and events from a women's point of view. Mrs. Annie Besant was the first President, Mrs. Dorothy Jinarjadasa was the secretary for eight years.

In 1929, an All India Conference was held at Pune to consider the reforms concerning social and educational problems. It was called as "The All India Women's Conference for Educational and Social Reforms". In December 1929, it met at Lahore. The Conference at Trivandrum met under the presidentship of Maharani of Travancore in 1935. Resolutions were passed urging vocational educations for women and national language for the entire country. The 16th All India Conference was held at Kakinada. Mrs. Vijayalaxmi Pandit presided over it. Resolution was passed to organise a women Volunteer Peace Corps. The first Asian Women's Conference was held at Lahore in 1931. It brought women leaders of Asia together. The headquarters was located at Egmore, Madras. It concentrated on compulsory elementary education, child marriage restraint, raising the age of consent and right to vote to women.

The Government of India appointed a committee on 22nd September, 1971 to inquire into the conditions of women, Report on measures to improve the status of women in India. The Committee submitted its Report on 31st Dec., 1971. It was published under the title "Towards Equality". The committee has recommended as many as 36 recommendations. In 1966, a resòlution was passed at Surat Conference requesting the government to institute a system of proper licensing for "Homes for Women and Children". In December, 1968, a seminar on uniform civil code was held at Chandigarh.

In 1969, the conference at Bangalore demanded in a resolution legilsation to secure for children, parental care, health services and nutrition, education and training. The A.I.W.C. hosted the 23rd Triennial Congress of International Alliance of Women in November, 1973. A.I.W.C. was reaffiliated to UNICEF it being the 95th N.G.O. on the "UNITED NATINS LIST". The National Federation of Indian Women (NFIW) was started in 1954 by communist minded women. N.F.I.W. is affiliated to Women's International Democratic Federation founded in 1943.

RESERVATION IN POLITICAL BODIES

(a) In Legislature and Parliament

The question whether there should be reserved places for women in the legislature has became controversial. The committee on the status of women in the India has gone into the question and received evidence. Opinion was divided on the issue.

(a) The reluctance of political parties to sponsor women candidates in sizable numbers leads to tokenism;

(b) If the present process continues there is the danger of more and more women opting out of political process;

(c) Women getting elected on reserved seats will ultimately become more articulated;

(d) Spokespersons of women's cause will increase;

(e) Improving the political status of women is an integral aspect of the overall problem of socio-economic change;

(f) Reservation of at least thirty per cent seats in legislative bodies will alter the very character of the legislature and will compel the political parties to change their strategies and induce them to give the women their due;

(g) Presence of more women in the legislature or parliament will help to direct the vote and type of change in the position of women;

(h) Such a measure will contribute to equality.

The Committee admitted that the problem under representation of women is representative bodies of the state both quantitatively and qualitatively is a real one. But still the committee rejected the suggestion for reservation in the legislature.

(b) Reservation of Seats for Women in Municipalities etc.

The Committee however pleaded for special opportunities for women for participation in the representative structure of local self government. They felt that it is time that we move out of this token provision for women's representation to a more meaningful association of women in the structure of local administration. It is pertinent to note that at present some seats are reserved for women in municipalities. There are provision for cooption of women in Zilla Parishads and mandals or panchayat samitis. The committee went to the extent of suggesting women's panchayats to administer women's measures.

The Committee also suggested to adopt definite policy regarding percentage of women candidates in the party. The Committee recommended inclusion of women in all important committee, commission or delegation.

WOMEN'S ASSOCIATION

(1) All India Women's Conference

A pamphlet "Women! know you rights" written by Shyamala Pappu and Kamala Ramji was published in 1976. A National Seminar on 'Family as the Foundation of National Development and Welfare' was held at Patna in 1977. A seminar on family planning was held at Delhi in 1980. Half yearly conference was held in May, 1982 at Gopenswar, U.P. The conference was disrupted at the increasing violence by Harijan Women. A seminar was held by the Ministry of Labour, Government of India on all India basis on 'Vocation Training for Women' in September, 1982. The A.I.W.C. participated in it.

Post Women's Decade from 1985

Essential nature of this period became noteworthy for the increasing atrocities on women, awareness of the same among women, legislative measures to counter them and steps taken by the women's association and women's movement to enhance the status of women in the society:

(i) Nairobi Conference was held in 19th July, 1985. It revitalised women's movement. It is left to the 'UN Committee on the Status of Women' to accelerate the raising of the status of women;

(ii) SAARC(South Asian Association for Regional Cooperation) countries have supported it. It strives for women's freedom. It agitates, educates and organises women;

(iii) All India Democratic Association of Women were mostly women of CPI (M) persuasion. It publishes a quarterly 'EQUALITY'. It gave a call for unity of women;

(iv) Young Women's Christian Association (YWCA) is an organization world wide of Christian women;

(v) Joint Action Programme has been concentrating its attention on unfortunate sisters of slum areas and poorer classes;

(vi) Mahila Dakshyata Samiti came into existence in 1977 and functioning ever since with its branches in Delhi, Andhra, Orissa, West Bengal, Maharastra, Himachal, Uttar Pradesh, Punjab and Chandigarh.

Many meeting were held, many seminars symposia were arranged. Government Department, Semi-Government Corporations, Local Self Governing Institutions, and International Agencies vied with one another in celebrating the year the year of the Girl Child i.e. from 1991 to 2000 A.D. by the S.A.A.R.C. Countries.

Constitutional Provisions Relating to the Rights of Women

The constitution of India has provided the directions and strategies for setting right the inequalities of the system firstly by guaranteeing certain fundamental rights to all its citizens and secondly, by directing the state to follow certain principles of state policy listed in the enactment of laws on various aspects of social and economic life in the country.

The main provisions of the Indian Constitution having bearing on women's social, economic and political status are summarised below:

Preamble

(a) To secure to all its citizens justice social, economic and political;

(b) Liberty of thought, expression, faith and worship;

(c) Equality of status and opportunity.

Fundamental Rights

Article-14

(i) Equality Before Law

The State shall not deny to any person equality before the law or the equal protection of the laws within the territory of India.

Article-15 (1)

(ii) Rights Against Discrimination

The state shall not discriminate against any citizen on grounds of religion, race, caste, sex, place of birth or any of them.

Article-15 (3)

Nothing in this Article shall prevent the state from making special provisions for women and children.

Article-16 (2)

(iii) Equality of Opportunity

No citizen shall on grounds only of religion, race, caste, sex, place of birth, be ineligible or discriminate against the respect of any employment or office under the state.

Article-21

(iv) Rights to Life and Personal Liberty

No person shall be deprived of his life or personal liberty, except according to procedure established by law.

DIRECTIVE PRINCIPLES OF STATE POLICY

Article-39

(i) *Certain Principles of Policy to be followed by the State*

The state shall in particular direct its policy towards securing:

(a) That the citizens, men and women equally, have the right to an adequate means of livelihood;

(b) That the health and strength of workers, man and women and the tender age of children are not abused;

(c) Right to work, to education, and to public assistance in some cases;

(d) The state shall make provisions for securing human conditions of work and for maternity relief.

International Level

India is a party to the U.N. Charter. Accordingly, it has already ratified several U.N. Covenants on the status of women. The human rights activities and those pursuing women's rights have also influenced both the government and women activists and those pursuing women's rights have also influenced both the government and women activists in India. Some of the conventions are listed below:

(a) The U.N. Declaration of Human Rights 1948 reaffirms the ideal of equal right of men and women;

(b) The preamble of the convention on political rights of women 1953, expressed its desired to equalise the status of men and women;

(c) The U.N. covenant on Economic social and Cultural Rights, 1956, exhorts that rights will be exercised without any discrimination of any kind;

(d) The International Covenants of Civil and Political Rights 1965 urges equal treatment of men and women;

(e) The convention on Elimination of All forms of Discrimination Against Women 1977 asserts that discrimination against women in violation of principles of equality of rights and respect for human dignity;

(f) Equal Remuneration Conventions of 1951 urges to ensure equal conditions of work and wages for men and women;

(g) Article 14 of the social policy convention 1962 reiterates the Principles of equality;

(h) Convention Against Discrimination in Education 1960 forbids discrimination on grounds of sex.

The sum and substance of all these U.N. Declaration and Covenants have their reflections not only in Indian Constitution but various statutes concerning their social and economic status, welfare and development. India's participation at several U.N. International and regional meets on women issues held in Mexico. Nairobi, SAARC have further helped to strengthen our resolve for creating conditions congenial to women's development thus taking suitable steps and measures to fulfill its aspirations of improving the status of Indian women, who have suffered discrimination for centuries.

Legislations About Women

Legislation and its implementation are elements not only in an organised society but is also indicative of the status of a society affords to its women. The main features of social legislation covering women are:

(a) To what extent it helps in removal of gender inequality?

(b) To what extent it succeeds in bringing about socio-economic changes?

(c) This would depend upon whether the socio-cultural factors have been taken into consideration while enacting laws and public opinion has been created in favour of particular law;

(d) Whether there is uniformity in the laws concerning all sections of a society and that these do not result in discrimination;

(e) Social organisation providing legal literacy and legal aid;

(f) Effectiveness of implementing machinery system and monitoring and review;

(g) Extent and frequency of amendments codification and enacting new laws to plug in the lacunae.

To revive the Panchayayati Raj institutions the 73rd and 74th amendments of the constitution were passed some time ago. Corresponding legislations were also enacted. They are extremely potent instruments of empowerment. These enactments *inter alia* provide for 33 per cent reservation of seats for women in the local, municipal and district bodies.

The Government needs to consider passing appropriate legislation applicable to all Indians which (1) All family assets and other properties like land and cultivation rights, tenancy right etc. acquired after marriage would be deemed to be jointly owned by both wife and husband (2) Every parent would deem to have made a will in which he or she has willed family assets equally to their beneficiaries. Unless a country's desire has been expressed in writing, giving valid reasons for doing, these laws would help the society eventually strike a balance for the enjoyment of the economic rights and appreciation of the role of women in the family.[12]

Civic Rights

Whereas we cannot accept the present basis of franchise, which restricts the number of enfranchised men and women specially the number of women to a small percentage of the total population and whereas we cannot accept the special qualification for women which requires them to be the wives of voters enfranchised on property qualification, the All India Women's Conference affirms that:

(a) Every man and women of twenty one and above unless otherwise disqualified shall have a right to vote in elections to the legislatures, central or provincial to municipalities and local bodies; and

(b) That women shall have a right to be represented in legislatures, municipalities, local bodies and all committees, conference, commissions or delegations that government may appoint or call whether for services at home or abroad.

The All India Women's conference demand that:

(a) The present system for education be overhauled and a system more suited to the needs and requirements of the country be adopted;

(b) No basic difference be made between the education of man and woman as their duties as citizens are the same;

(c) The (1) Pre-basic, (2) Basic (3) Secondary (4) Vocational (5) University (6) Adult Education form an integral part of the system of education and the medium of instruction through the recognised language on the province;

(d) Basic education be a seven year's course and be made free and compulsory for every boy and girl from the age of seven to the age of fourteen;

(e) In view in particular of the lack of teachers, equipment and buildings, co-education be adopted in all stages, with a possible exception in the secondary stage until prejudice against it has been overcome;

(f) The government shall through legislation if necessary make immediate efforts to eradicate the evils of child marriage, child labour, purdah and untouchability which came in the way of education and specially of girl's education;

(g) The Government shall give aid to such poor parents as are reluctant to send their girls to schools for economic reasons by awarding scholarship to the girls, providing books and materials free and by such other means;

(h) The Government shall help the brighter and more intelligent girls who should continue their studies even after the compulsory period is over and who are unable to do so for financial reasons by providing scholarships, freeships, books and by such other means;

(i) Physical education through exercise and games, education for health shall form part of the school curricula;

(j) Secondary education shall be as varied circumstances permit and shall not be unduly restricted by the requirement of universities or examining bodies;

(k) A large number of secondary schools shall be provided so that such education may be within the reach of everyone who needs it;

(l) In order to facilitate vocational education among women, there shall be provision for polytechnics on an extensive scale;

(m) Regional universities shall be established soon that more men and women can take advantage of higher education;

(n) Education in art, music and home science shall form part of the University curricula;

(o) Hostels shall be provided to facilitate women joining the various education institutions either as students or teachers;

(p) There shall be a large number of institutions for training of women teachers to meet the growing need and free scholarships are to be provided to induce more women to take the training and that refresher course for teachers be provided at regular intervals;

(q) The status of teachers shall be raised in order to attach the better educated women by improving the conditions of their service, providing *inter alia* for better pay, free housing, and a social insurance scheme which would include maternity benefits;

(r) Primary schools, secondary schools and other educational institutions shall be housed in their own buildings;

(s) Special facilities for the education of adult women in rural areas shall be provided by Government such as residential schools for adults on the lines of the folk schools in Denmark;

(t) Health education including nutrition and citizenship shall form part of the curricula of adult education and mobile exhibitions with competent lectures who would demonstrate on all matters pertaining to village life including model homes, hygiene, sanitation, care of children, kitchens, gardens etc. be organised;

(u) Every village with a school shall have a library and reading room; and

(v) The government and municipalities shall actively help in the cultural education of the people by establishing central libraries, art galleries, museums and national theatres in order to enable them to make wise use of leisure.

II. Health

Whereas the health of every man, women and child is the nation's greatest asset and whereas conditions in this country are such that they have undermined the health of the peoples as can be seen from the appalling death rate and the figures for maternal and infant mortality and whereas these conditions must be improved, the All India Women's Conference demands that:

(a) A nation-wide plan of free health services, including medical, dental and hospital treatment and provision for free medical examination be adopted;

(b) A nation-wide plan of free pre-natal and infant welfare clinics, maternal hospitals and nursing services be adopted;

(c) All preventive measures such as medical inspection of school children, child welfare centers, sanitation, general hygiene, industrial hygiene and immunisation services be taken;

(d) More facilities for the training of men and women doctor as well as health visitors be provided;

(e) Steps be taken to popularize the profession of nursing in order to induce more women to join in and the conditions of service of the nurses and the probationers who are under training be improved by way of adequate housing, pay and allowances, regulating hours of work, facilities for recreation, holidays with pay and social insurance;

(f) The training in nursing be given through the medium of a recognised provincial language;

(g) The public be educated to recognise the early signs of disease such as tuberculosis, cancer, leprosy and venereal disease;

(h) Adequate facilities be provided for the segregation and free treatment of infectious diseases including leprosy and venereal diseases;

(i) The government or local bodies concerned shall take steps for the provision of a clean water supply and drainage system as well as for the proper disposal of rural and urban areas;

(j) Overcrowding in houses be stopped by law;

(k) The Government shall take steps to improve the bad housing in urban as well as rural areas.

III. Moral Standards

Social conditions and the chronic economic distress in this country have raised an ugly problems *viz.*, the traffic in women and children. Advantage is taken of the helplessness of women destitute to entice them for immoral purpose. The All-India women's conference, therefore, demand that:

(a) There shall be an equal moral standards for men and women;

(b) Rescue homes on scientific lines be established to rehabilitate women who have been victims of the evils;

(c) Rules and regulations be framed for the conduct of homes and hostel meant for women so that no nefarious practice may be carried on under the guise of running such homes; and

(d) Steps be taken to improve the social and economic conditions of the people in order to minimise and eventually eradicate the evil.

IV. Work

Whereas in a democratic state the right to work is a fundamental right of every individual whether man or woman; and whereas no disability should attach to men on the ground of her sex in regard to public employment, office of power or in the exercise of any trade or calling ; and whereas woman must receive the same payment as men for the same amount of work she does, the All India Women's Conference demands that:

(a) There shall be no bar to the employment of married or unmarried women provided they are prepared to abide by the conditions of service;

(b) No women shall be debarred owing to sex from the enjoyment of full equality regarding social and labour rights and duties, but both men and women shall equally receive special consideration on grounds of health and in the case of women on ground of motherhood.

(c) While women workers shall have the same facilities as men workers with regard to pay which should be living wage, leave hours of work, sickness allowance, holidays with pay and free medical treatment; and shall have the same amenities with regard to bathrooms, lavatories, canteens serving hot meals etc. they shall be allowed special facilities by way of:

1. Creches for their babies and Nursery schools;
2. Rest rooms for expectant and nursing mothers;
3. Milk canteen for the children, nursing and expectant mothers;
4. A break during work for expectant and nursing mothers; and
5. Maternity benefits which shall form part of a comprehensive scheme of social insurances.

Home Making

Whereas the work of the housewife has so far received no recognition in the sense that no steps have been taken or contemplated for the protection of one who works from morning till night without rest or leave on holiday ; and whereas we believe the work of a housewife to be as important as any other, we deem it essential, in the interest of these women who are the home makers and the mother of the race, that steps be taken for the raising of their status for the protection of their health and for providing leisure in order to enable them to improve their mind and the All India women's conference. Therefore demands that:

(a) The husband shall have no right to dispose of his entire property without consent of his wife;

(b) The woman who works in the home shall have a right to a part of her husband's income to be sued by her as she likes;

(c) If any scheme of social insurance that the Government may introduce for the benefit of the workers who works outside home such as workers in their fields of factories, teachers or nurses, the home-maker shall be included for purposes of benefit and any contribution to be made to the fund shall be deducted from the husband's income if the wife has no separate income of her own;

(d) Creches, infant classes and pre-basic schools shall be provided by the government or municipalities; and

(e) Facilities shall be provided for the women to learn how to run her home in a systematic and scientific way.

VI. Property Right

Whereas, we believe that woman should have the same rights as man to hold, acquire inherit and dispose of property; and whereas some of those rights are denied to woman or if given are on unequal basis, the All India Women's Conference demands that:

(a) The sex disqualification by which women have hitherto been precluded from inheriting in various parts of India be removed;

(b) Women shall inherit in her absolute right; and

(c) There shall no discrimination between sons and daughters, that in both shall have equal share in the property of their father or mother.

VII. Whereas we believe that the marriage laws in this country are one-sided and have made the lives of many women unbearable, the All India Women's Conference demand that the laws be improved and changed to suit modern conditions of life by providing that:

(a) No marriage shall take place if either the girl is below the age of 16 or the boy is below the age of 21;

(b) Neither party shall have a husband or wife living at the time of marriage;

(c) The consent of both the parties concerned shall be necessary before their marriage;

(d) There shall be restriction to marriage on the grounds of caste or community; and no declaration shall be necessary to renounce their religion before two persons can marry;

(e) Either party shall have the right to dissolve the marriage under certain conditions including cruelty, desertion for 3 years, suffering from incurable disease and impotency;

(f) Such cases of divorce shall be conducted in camera before a special matrimonial court;

(g) A wife who has obtained a divorce from her husband be entitled to claim alimony from him until such time as she marries again.

The initial recognition of women's rights which emerged during the freedom struggle and was expressed in the constitution has vanished into the thin air. Indian society's inherent male chauvinism among the most distressing facts of life that has not changed with freedom.

The latest legislation passed by the parliament in the interest of projecting the status of Indian women in the indecent representation of women (prohibition) Act 1986. The Act prohibits sale, distribution, circulation of any books, pamphlets, and depicting indecent portrayal of women. It is however strange that this law does not intend to impose strict censorship on cinema which has taken the lead in representing women in many derogatory way as applicable. In fact, the law relating to obscenity in India is already codified in section 292, 293 and 294 of the Indian Penal Code but these provisions have seldom been implemented.[13]

The Constitution of India has not only provided for equal rights and privileges as between men and women but has given and gone a step further and made special provisions for women through social justice and equality of status and opportunity are the signs of the constitution.[14]

The Supreme Court has given a new thrust the human rights of women who have been victims of crime since time immemorial. By ordering prosecution of former Punjab Police Chief K.P.S. Gill for allegedly outraging the modesty of an women I.A.S. Officer, Rupam Deol Bajaj, the apex court asserted its power for protection of personal liberty of the weaker vessel.

In a step towards gender equality, the apex court has held that state is competent to give preference to women in government jobs where they are equally meritorious but more suited than men.

It is not out of place to mention that the idea of equality is a modern concept. Women all over the world do appear to have secure formal legal equality and political emancipation. The moment they were entitled to the right to vote and active participation in politics and nation building exercises. Those drafting the Indian constitution were associated with the emancipation of women.

Women and Child Development Department, Government of Orissa has been created as a separate department since 1994-95. The objectives of this department is to safeguard the interest and to implement different development schemes for children, women, old, handicapped and people of poor classes. For women welfare it has done the following works:

(A) Dowry Prohibition Scheme

In order to eradicate the evils of dowry, the state governments has encouraged NGOs to organise dowryless marriages, anti-dowry campaigns, seminars and workshops etc. During 1995-96 funds to the extent of Rs. 25,000/- has been sanctioned in favour of different organisations for organising 5 numbers of anti-dowry seminars and workshops. A sum of Rs. 50,000/- has been allotted for the year 1996-97 in this scheme.

(B) Working Women's Hostels

In order to provide accommodation for working women Government of India introduced with 75 per cent held for construction of working hostel as grant in aid. Till the end of last year 11 working women's hostels were constructed which includes 690 seats. Funds to the extent of Rs. 5.00 Lakhs was provided under State Plan Budget during 1995-96 for the purpose and a sum of Rs. 5.00 Lakhs is provided in 1996-97 financial year in this scheme.

(C) State Commission for Women

The State Commission for women, Orissa has been constituted in 1992-93 in order to prohibit of Dowry death and eradication of atrocities on women and taking up the following works like marriage and dowry, rape, kidnapping etc. In order to educate women against the above evils the books named "Jautak Ayen Amara Kartabya. Hindu Bibha Ayen eka Surakhya Kabacha O Subha Shanketa" etc. have been distributed among the NGOs, Collector and women colleges. District level seminars have been organised. Last year the commission has taken up 4,940 different cases from which 343 spot enquiries were held and action were taken on 4918 cases. A sum of Rs. 15 Lakhs were spent in last year and a sum of Rs. 5 Lakhs has been provided in the budget for 1996-97.

(D) Mahila Vikas Samabaya Nigam

Since 1990-91 the M.V.S.N. is working as the apex Women Cooperative Society getting the financial help from the Nigam. During 1995-96 a provision of Rs. 9.00 lakh was spent and a sum of Rs. 9 Lakhs has been provided during the year 1996-97.

(E) Rehabilitation of Women in Distress

In order to rehabilitate the women in distress vocational training in different trades have been provided by this department. A sum of Rs. 3.61 Lakhs had been spent and 310 women were benefited during Seventh Plan period in the scheme. During 1995-96 a sum of Rs. 6 Lakhs have been spent to benefit 275 women. A sum of Rs. 6 Lakhs have been provided during 1996-97 in the scheme.

There are a large number of laws for women which are being amended and new laws continue to be made. India perhaps has the largest number of laws for women. The government has taken a lot of interest and shown a lot of concern for women and women's issue. What is not needed is that parliament, the government, the advocates and judiciary interpret laws in favour of women. In this connection, mention must be made of the judgment of Justice Aggarwal, Additional District and Sessions Judge, Tis Hazari. His landmark judgements have had far reaching consequences leading to amendments in law in favour of women. He was the first to give a life sentence to a rapist.

There is a definite need to analyse the laws and their weak implementation to actually find out as to where the difficulty in implementation lies. When an attempt is made, it would be revealed that absence of support from the families/community has definitely been responsible for weak implementation of laws. Dissemination of updated information on laws through newsletters, pamphlets, posters will prove to be useful to girls/women. Simple posters could be displayed in all schools, colleges, universities and office (both in English and the regional language of the area. Display will create an awareness among the teachers, students, parents and the Public. The community and the NGOs must work together to organise meetings and workshops on women and law and work out strategies for providing free legal aid. Both the community and the NGOs must have a social binding on them for taking up women's issues seriously and genuine:

(i) Aminocentesis/Infanticide

(ii) Dowry demands/dowry deaths

(iii) Compulsory education of girls

(iv) Helping women in distress

(v) Ill-treatment by husbands/families

(vi) Ill-treatment by sons, daughter-in-law

(vii) Young widows

To ensure that laws actually help women it is important that women themselves become aware of their rights, the families and the community help in the internationalisation of laws and the legal aid for women in the courts becomes more effective.[15]

There is no denying the fact that women in our days have begun to acquire the status of equality with men and several arena till recently closed for women have opened their gates to them. Nevertheless struggle for complete emancipation and equality goes on. In the context, judiciary through rulings and interpretation has helped women.

The picture can change only if women of all categories join hands to effectively fight for their socio-economic and cultural rights as well as for the most fundamental rights of their dignity and honour. Enlightened men should also abandon their misplaced chauvinism and support the cause of suffering and deprived women.[16]

REFERENCES

1. *Status of Women in Khurda District:* A Synopsis of the Status Report. A study Undertaken by Khuda District Action Group (KAG) in Collaboration with Centre for Development Research and Training, 1996.
2. Pandey Mrinal, *"Gender, Poverty and Cats on a Pilgrimage"* Mainstream, Vol. XXX, No. 24, April 14, 1992.
3. Krishna Raj Maithreyi, *Women and Development, The Indian Experience*, Shubhad Saraswat Prakashan, Pune, 1988, pp. 20-22.
4. George J, *"Adjustment with Gender Equity"*, Mainstream, Vol. XXX 1, No. 20, March, 27, 1993.
5. Sahaya Kumud, *Women in Focus, A Community in Search of Equal Roles*, Sangam Books (India) Pvt. Ltd., 1984.
6. Sapru R.K., *Women and Development*, Ashish Publishing House, New Delhi, 1989, p. 315.
7. Jha, Ajit Kumar *"Women, Saga of Struggle"*, Civil Service Chronicle, April, 1996.
8. Ahuja Ram, *The Rights of Women: A Feminist Perspective*, Rawat Publications, New Delhi, 1984.
9. Mrs. (Singh K.P.), *"Women and Development: Gender Concerns"* in the Book, P.N. Pimpley, K.P. Singh, A. Mahajan (edc.), Social Development. Process and Consequences, Rawat Publications, Jaipur, 1989, pp. 89-90.
10. Chowdhury, D.Paul, *Women's Welfare and Development*. A Source Book, India Publication, New Delhi, 1992.
11. Devender Kiran, *Changing Status of Women In India*, Vikas Publishing House Pvt. Ltd., New Delhi, 1994, p. XII.
12. Khan Sona's Article *"New Laws for Higher Status"* in the Indian Express, Vizianagaram, 15th Jan., 1996.
13. Devendra Kiran, *Changing Status of Women in India*, Vikas Publishing House Pvt. Ltd., New Delhi, 1994.
14. Rashtriya Sahara, April, 1995, p. 129.
15. Devendra Kiran, *Changing Status of Women in India*, Vikas Publishing House, Pvt. Ltd., New Delhi, 1994.
16. Mohan Inder, *"Just An Ideal Still"*, Hindustan Times, 15th October, 1992.

6

PARTICIPATION OF WOMEN IN POLITICS
A STUDY IN ORISSA

Dr. NILANCHAL MUNI*

Women have long been a suppressed group. In all sphere of life men have systematically dominated them. The subjugation of women by men is not confined only to developing countries. This is also present though to a lesser degree in most developed countries. However, since the last few years's women's liberation movement has gained some momentum in western countries. Their spill over effect in developing countries does not appear to be significant. It is thus apparent that the level of development of country is correlated with the status of women in their country. A corollary of this hypothesis is that the nature of women participation in politics is greatly affected by the level of development of a country. Further, the socio-economic status of a woman tends to affect her political participations.

Indian history provides a few examples of Indian women having excellent as ruler and statesman. But by and large, our women used to fight taking part in politics. In fact, political participation by then started during the Indian Freedom Struggle. Mahatma Gandhi was a strong advocate of female participation

* **Lecturer in Pol. Science, K.S.U.B.College, Bhanjnagar, Ganjam.**

in polities[1]. Our independence movement produced some eminent women leaders like Annie Basant, Sarojini Naidu, Durg Bai etc.

The present studies have dealt with the nature of participation of women in Orissa Assembly election.

Rapid expansion of communication, education industrialisation and urbanisation seems to have brought about some changes in the attitude and outlook of Indian women[2]. They have to some extent been modernised. But they have been fully free of the cultural values and more of Indian. Empirical evidence suggest that Indian women in general one political much less active than Indian men[3]. It has been further said that the spread of literacy and mass communication motivate women to be interested and active in politics[4] these forces tend to stimulate their political awareness. In India, Orissa happens to be one of the poorest state with a semi feudal economy and a predominantly conservative culture. To a great extend conservatism in Orissan society of its feudal economy. The domination of one class by another class has resulted in the domination of one caste by another caste and the domination of women by men. Throughout our history man has occupied the central stage while the woman has been forced to perish in the wings. The leadership and authority structures have mostly been dominated by men who have through ancient traditions forced women to remain under purdah.

In the pre-independence Orissa politics it was found that non of the three ministries of Orissa of the period (1936-1947) included a single women member. Further, still more important to note is that not a single woman was elected to the Orissa Legislative Assembly from a general constituency.

But after India become independent there was some increase in the political participation of woman. In Orissa, a few women have become ministers but for one there were not very influential. For a long time the Orissa Politics was dominated by male leaders like H.K. Mahatab, Biju Pattanik, R.N.Singh Deo, Biren Mitra, J.B.Pattnaik, Naveen Pattanik, Smt. Basant Manjari Devi the "Queen" of Ranpur was first appointed as a Deputy Minister and then a Minister of Health. But she was not an important political leader of the state.

It was only in 1970s that there was some change in the political balance between men and women in Orissa. Mrs. Nandini Satpathy who was a Minister of state of the center was sent by Mrs. Indira Gandhi to Orissa as the Chief Minister on 1972. Mrs. Satpathy was an effective administrator and a strong politician. But her political supremacy did not signify any significant women power in Orissa politics.

Between 1952-1990 only a small number of woman have been elected to the Orissa Legislative Assembly while in 1952 there were 2 women MLAs in 1980 it was 5 in 2000, it was 11 and in 2005 it was 13. Thus, there has not been a steady and significant increase in the number of women MLAs between 1952 and 2005.

Different empirical survey reflects that the Oriya women MLAs elected so far mostly belong to the elite castes of the state. As a single group the Kshatriya caste (connected with "royal" houses) has contributed the largest number of women MLAs. The apparent dominance of Kshatriya women over other women in the filed of politics is primary due to the feudal background and nature of the state.

It is important to note that up to 1971 a singe Brahmin women could be elected as an MLA even though it is one of the dominant caste of the state. It was only in 1972 that Mrs. Satpathy a Brahmin was elected to the Legislative assembly. The Karans and Khandayats, the other two caste groups placed lower in the social hierarchy up to 1990 assembly election so far women politics in Orissa is concerned. The number of women MLA was increased in 2000 assembly election up to 11(eleven) though the number was not impressive in comparison to the total strength of the Orissa Assembly. Still then they were inspired land conscious to fight for their own causes. At the same time for Schedule Tribe 1980 was very important because four women MLAs were elected form their Reserved constituency. However, in 2000 and 2005 Assembly election the number of women MLAs have been increased and some of them were also inducted in the ministry as state minister.

The elitist nature of women politics in Orissa indicates that some women leaders as been elected more than once to the legislative assembly. Some of them were Nandini Satpathy, Sugyani Kumari Devi, Draupadi Murmu, Bijaya Laxmi Sahu.

Women participation in politics is more in coastal districts rather than the hill districts. There are some hill districts like Phulbani, Koraput, Keonjhar, Balangir which have never sent a women MLA to the state legislature, Cuttack which is the most developed district in the state has the pride of sending the highest number of women MLAs to the Orissa Legislative Assembly. So the regional imbalance in respect of over all development between the coastal and hill districts is reflected in their respective success in electing women MLAs.

Orissa is predominantly a Hindu Province, the number of Muslims who are concentrated in a few pockets like Cuttack and Bhadrak is negligible. The strength of Christians is not significant from the election point of view. It is thus not a surprise not a single Muslim or Christian women from Orissa has so far been elected to the state legislature.

Thus, in this respect the picture in Orissa is much different from that of Assam which is a multi religious and multi-lingual state. In Assam women legislators elected so far include quite a significant number of Bengali speaking and Muslim women[5].

Conclusion

Feudal economy coupled with conservatism and feudal values have resulted in the dominance of women by men of centuries. The women liberation movement has made some progress in western countries. But its impact in developing continued to be a subjugated group with their social and political freedom greatly inhibited and restricted by social "laws".

The women participation in politics in Orissa was increased after independence. By a small number they were elected to state legislature and to the sense of them were appointed as ministers. However, in the restricted sense of political participation that is in respect of representation in legislatures, and women is almost as wide as ever. Further the women political activists of Orissa both before 1947 and after it mostly belong to the elite structure of society. A few women of the "Depressed Communities" who have managed to be elected to the state legislature have returned only from reserved constituencies[6].

REFERENCES

1. M.K.Gandhi, Women and Social Justice (Bombay 1947).

   M.K.Gandhi, The Role of Women, (Bombay,1964).

2. Pramila Kapur, Studies on the Urban Women in India, Giri Raj Gupta Edited, Family and Social Change in Modern India (New Delhi, 1976), pp. 66-102.

3. C.P. Bhambri and P.S.Verma, The Urban Voter, (New Delhi, 1973), p. 78.

4. Status of Women in India, ICSSR (New Delhi 1975), pp. 105-107.

5. N.Hazarika, "Role of Women in State Politics of Assam", India Journal of Political Science, Vol. 39, No. 1 , Jan.-March 1978, pp. 61-78.

6. Report of Orissa Legislative Assembly, 2005.

7

WOMEN POLITICS
AN ILLUSION

Dr. BISHNU NARAYANA SETHI*

The strengthening of women's participation in all spheres of life has become a major issue in the discourse of economic and social development in the last decades virtually every international and bilateral development agency has proclaimed policies to integrate women better into economic and social process. The promotion of women in politics however , especially if it is supposed to be implemented through affirmative action is still contested. This is in spite of the fact that women from around 50 per cent of total world population share a considerable laws presence in elected political bodies.

The empowerment and autonomy of women and the improvement of women's social , economic and political status is essential for achievement of transparent accountable government, administration and sustainable development in all area of life. In every society, there are powerful and powerless groups. Power itself can be simply defined as control over resources and control of ideology and it is exercise through a series of order or decision making capacity. The resources over which control can be exercised fall into five broad categories such as physical resources, human

* **Lecturer in Economics, Researcher ICSSR, HRD , New Delhi.**

resources, intellectual resources, financial resources and self. Similarly, control of ideology mean the ability of determined belief, values attitudes and virtual control over way of thinking and situational . Those who have powers are those who control material knowledge, resources and the ideology, which govern both public and private life and these are in a position to make decision which benefit themselves . The extent of power of an individual or group is in turn correlated to how many different kind of resources they can access and control. This control confers decision-making power which is used to increase access to and control over resources. If the above definition is accepted then it is clear that women is general and poor women in particulars are relatively powerless because they do not have control over resources and hence little or no decision making.

Social Roles

Society has institutionalised a sharp demarcation of social roles according to sex in which are half of its members voluntarily accept a role subordinate to the other half. The fact that such a division of labour extending into both economic and political spheres has existed throughout history and in most area of the world doesn't lesson the impact of such a secondary role as women. Men virtually monopolise the high status of positions of decision making and formulation of goals in major economic, political and cultural institution of society. The rationale , such as it is for this perception stresses that women want it that way, supported by studies which show that women are relatively a political , women prefer the domestic sphere, of home and family and thus choose to leave political and civic affair to man. This rises the question whether it is traditional feminine values and sex stereotyping which causes women to lower own separation not only with respect to social roles, but also within the full spectrum of political attitudes and participation. If an interrelatedness between traditional feminine values, sex stereotyping and political awareness could be demonstrated it might serve to explain the well known myths of women's preconceived attitude and pattern of behaviour.

It is surprising that political scientists have excluded women as deserving major concern and attention few little effort have been made to question the widely held belief that politics is strictly a masculine affairs and that women's place is in the home. On the contrary the profession evaded the question be relying one cultural gender role definition for the status of women in politics rather than actually investigating the nature of status . The lower status of women in politics has been perpetuated and accepted because culture contrived and supported the myth of inferiority of women and their unsuitability to take up politics. Men's role revolves around his occupation, the women's around her family.

Women in Politics

The traditional working pattern of many political parties and government structures continue to be barriers to women's participation in public life. Women may be discouraged from seeking political office by discriminatory attitudes and practices family and child-care responsibility and the high cost of seeking and holding public office.

Political parties are the articulated organisation of active political agents who are concerned with the control of global powers and who compete for popular support with another group or groups. As a result political parties are the great intermediaries linking the social forces and ideologies to official government institutions and relating them to political action within the community. Political parties chalk out programmes broad enough to cover the entire range of political activity and make the issues and interest known to mass. They disseminate the value of the political system and mobilise public opinion for political action. Thus, the stimulate to participate are provided by political parties.

Women in politics and decision-making positions in government and legislative bodies contribute to redefining political priorities placing new items on the political agenda that reflect and address women's gender-specific concerns values and experiences and providing new perspectives an mainstream politics issues.

Political status of women can be defined as the degree of equality and freedom enjoyed by women in the shaping and sharing of power and in the value by society to this role of women. The Indian constitution guarantees political equality through the adult franchise and the right to equality which prohibits discrimination on the ground of sex. The equal political status will not be realised by mere declaration in the constitution.

Political Profile of Women

Voting in the election does not bestow equal status. If adequate opportunities to take part in the deliberation of the nation are not provided participation has no meaning . The socio-economic conditions are not conducive for the effective participation of women in political affairs. Political equality is meaningless in a country where the mass of the population suffers from poverty, illiteracy, inequality of class status and power. Apart from these , women suffers from traditional attitudes, which made them to feel that they are unequal.

The political background of women show that they are far away from an equal status along with men. Women are politically not active and do not come forward to participate in the public affairs. The organisation exercise of franchise discussing politics etc. explains the political profile of the women.

The problem of equal status and equal participation must be understood in the context of a society in a traditional society like India the participation of women in public life is not encouraging since women are keeping low profile as far as political life is concerned.

Though women become member of political parties their percentage is very low when the question of closeness to political parties comes there also the picture is not too encouraging . Apart from political activities the part played by women in other social activities is minimal.

Ratio of Women in Politics

Women's representation have not excluded eight per cent any time in parliament . The Indian state has attempted to reduce this gap by the method of reservation at the local level bodies of self governance *i.e.* Panchayats through constitution (73rd Amendment Act , 1992) and through the 81 Amendment bill and Reservation of Women in parliament and Legislature women face when functioning a male dominated public forums, constraints that the result both from initial handicaps that women suffer because of their social conditioning and from male responses to their presence on those bodies pressures to prove themselves and constraints that emerge from their class and caste position. But again these handicaps through real in many cases, actually call for greater support from active women's and other progressive organisations to help women overcome these obstacles.

Even in the reservation provided by the new Panchayat Act, constitution amended as per 73rd Women presidents or Chairman are reluctant to discharge their function, in case where they are already always guided rather superseded by their spouses. They are obliged to have their spouses as back seat drivers in discharging their functioning.

Lack of proper education and necessary orientation also serves as hurdle for their effective functioning.

Social obligation, and traditional control of womenfolk by family members and their commitment to household work also serve, obstacles in permitting the women representatives to function effectively.

Reservation given to Scheduled Caste (SC) women or General women also suffers due to lack of committed representatives for the above said factors.

Hence the need of the hour to empower womenfolk is to provide necessary political education and proper orientation. Further political will and the part of administrators to contain male domination and enlarge avenues for the women just by negating gender weakness may help to a large extent in the empowerment of women.

Women Powers

Women should realise their potent power which is quite latent for long . They must be required to see themselves and their rights in a new way and they must be helped to help themselves. For this several non-government organisations run by women thousands of Mahila Mandals and Lakhs of women members in

Panchayati Raj Institutions should work towards sensitising other women by spreading awareness about their rights and the means by which they could be realised. They should mobilise and organise women as a strong pressure group to participate vigorously in the development process and decision-making. Further, the local level women's group need to be strengthened and empowered for the effective implementation of the programmes.

Women will need to work persistently and consistently at the national, State District and Village levels to understand the Policy process make them head of the relevant bodies and monitor the adopted plans. Further empowerment is about choices and the ability to exercise them. Women's choices will be limited unless they are more involved in policy making.

Conclusion

Women's group and women's movement have approached the state and pressurised it to frame pro women policy while the state has framed seemingly pro women policies these have actually helped to break sexual stereo type and male dominance either of these policies has been able to achieve the objective of equality and development. Thus women continue to have contradictory experiences will regard to the state policies. This rises the question as to how women should relate to state and what strategies should be adopted towards the state on account of the unwillingness of the state to change the status quo to genuinely help women doubts have been raised as to whether any more demands should be made to the state for more policies. It has been observed that due to various reasons the state has reserved to symbolic political and electoral consideration. The state has regretted to symbolic policy making and in the process has co-opted women's movement vocabulary terminology and agenda without bringing in any real changes in the lives of women. While this has provided the state with a pro-women image, it has a depoliticising effect on the movement. These are real problems with regards to the states dealing with women issues.

The strategies described above should really empowers women and bring them into the mainstream development. If employment , income and social security were improved, women should automatically become economically strong which will lead them to become powerful forces in contributing to the social and economic development of India.

REFERENCES

1. Kumar, Ashok and Harish , *Women Power: Status of Women in India* Gian Publishing House, New Delhi 1991.
2. Patri, Sushila, *Women Political Elite*: Search for Identity, Printwell, Jaipur-1994.
3. Shanti , K. (Ed.) *Empowerment of Women*, Anmol Publishing Private Limited , New Delhi-1998.
4. S.K. Ghose, *Women in a Changing Society*, Ashish Publishing House, New Delhi-1984.
5. Jane S. Jaquette, *Women in Politics* , New York John Wiley and Son-1979.

8

THE SOCIO-ECONOMIC AND POLITICAL STATUS OF INDIAN WOMEN

NIRANJAN PRADHAN*

"O woman: Lovely woman:

Nature made thee to temper man:

We had been beasts without you"

Otway

One of the Mahatma's visions was the empowerment of women in a tradition ridden mindset. That mindset remains today- and must be upgraded. The status of Indian women is not very high despite being revered as "goddess" and "Shakti" personified. She may be the embodiment of power of Shakti but being controlled by man. So woman loses her individuality, her very right to exist for herself. She is to be protected by her father in her youth, by her husband after marriage and by son in her old age. These ideas caused irreparable harm to the position of women in society.

The dawn of the nineteenth century witnessed the birth of a new vision. The Indian society at that period was caught in a

* **Research Scholar, Department of Political Science, Berhampur University, Orissa.**

serious grip created by religious superstitions and social obscurantism. The most distressing was women's position. The birth of a girl child creates a deep sense of grief among the family members, her marriage is an insoluble burden and her widowhood inauspicious. Attempts to kill female infants at birth were usual. The major effect of national awakening in the 19th century was seen especially in the field of social reforms. The one of the main objectives of social reforms was emancipation of women and extension of equal rights to them.

Social Status of Indian Women

Women were generally accorded a low status and were considered to be inferior to their male counterparts with no identity of their own. Their talents and hidden potentialities was suppressed by practices such as early marriage, ban on widow remarriage, practice of sati etc. Both the Hindus and Muslims women were economically and socially dependent, while education was generally denied to them. The Hindu women had no right to inherit property. Polygamy was prevalent among both Hindus as well as Muslims. The condition of upper class women was in this respect worse than that of peasant women. Man still continues to dominate over woman, and retains many privileges to himself. Meet the women of any class or creed whether they belong to lower class or middle class or upper class; everywhere there is "male dominance". Legal guardianship of adult women has been abolished; erosion in the economic guardianship has also started. But intellectual, emotional and social guardianship still exercises a stronghold upon them. The discrimination attitude towards women has adversely affected man-woman relations.

According to Prof. Amartya Sen, disadvantages of women are not; of course, unique to India, and there is much evidence of extensive gender based inequality even in the elementary matters of healthcare and nutrition in many regions across the world. But fairly detailed comparisons of mortality rates, morbidity rates, hospital care, nutritional attention etc. have been made in India, and they clearly confirm a fairly decisive future for women being systematically deprived vis-à-vis men in much of the country, especially rural India.

Women constitute half of the world's population, perform nearly two-thirds of its work hours, receive one-tenth of the world's income and own less than one hundredth of the world's property. Although Female literacy in the country has risen upto 54.16 per cent in 2001, compared to 21.97 per cent in 1971, it has continued to be below male literacy. Violence against women and girls is widely prevalent in different parts of India. In present day context, there has been an alarming growth of atrocities against women and children. To quote from the Encyclopaedia of women in South Asia.

In every 34 minutes a rape takes place. Every 42 minutes a sexual harassment incident occurs. Every 43 minutes a woman is kidnapped. And in every 93 minutes a woman is burnt to death for dowry. One fourth of the reported rapes involve girls under the age of 16 but the vast majorities are never reported.

The preference for boys over girls has resulted in the growth of infanticide and sex-selective abortion cases. This has created imbalance in the sex ratio of the nation. In 1971, there were 930 Females of every 1000 males. This figure increased to 934 in 1981. But this ratio started declining in 1991. As per the 2001 census the sex-ratio is 933. In most of the rural communities illegal child marriages still take place. The census of 2001 has brought out that for the first time, the sex ratio for children under six years (1971) has gone below the sex ratio for the total population (1932): this being largely the effect of female foeticide. Similarly, in spite of all efforts, female literacy has remained low in some states. Fatehgarh Saheb district in Punjab has lowest Fmr-6, namely 745 with Punjab as the epicenter, there is a continuous stretch encompassing Haryana, Delhi, Gujarat, Rajasthan, Maharashtra and western U.P that needs to be watched out for low Fmr. Policies like gender-desegregated census analysis of children below one year, more frequent census, village-wise analysis and stricter registration of ultra-sonography clinics need to be pursued. In the east, with Bihar as the epicenter, there is a continuous stretch econompassing the districts of Bihar, Jharkhand, eastern U.P Assam, Orissa, MP, and Andhra Pradesh where female literacy is low and the efforts for girl child education need to be strengthened. Many states show a typical trend wherein the districts with higher female literacy have lower Fmr-6. These points to a need for a paradigm shift in our educational value system.

Apparently it would be expected that Fmr should increase with the increase in education. The actual trends are quite the reverse. In orissa, the lowest literacy rate is 18 in the district of Nabarangpur. In Kerala, the lowest literacy rate is as high as 70 in Kasargod district.

Undoubtedly the education is the cornerstone of women's empowerment because it provides them to respond to opportunities, to challenge their traditional roles and to change their lives.

Table 8.1

Literacy rates in India

Census Year	*Persons*	*Males*	*Females*	*Male-Female app. in Literacy rate*
1951	18.33	27.16	8.86	18.30
1961	28.30	40.40	15.35	25.05
1971	34.45	45.96	21.97	23.98
1981	43.57	56.38	29.76	26.62
1991	52.21	64.13	39.29	29.84
2001	65.38	75.85	54.16	21.70

Steps Taken to Ameliorate the Plight of Women

March 8, is celebrated every year as international women's day. It focuses global attention on plight of the women in various regions. It reiterates the areas in which the lot of women still needs improvement, *viz.*, Female infanticide, child marriage, dowry, sexual harassment at workplaces, gender discrimination, etc.

Indian constitution guarantees equal rights of men and women. Despite the advances made by women in many fields, women's concerns are still not the foremost priority. They continue to face the discrimination and marginalisation, both subtle and blatant and don't share the permit of development equally. Though women have done excellent jobs in different walks of life and proved their talents yet an equal status is denied to them. Women like Sarojini Naidu, Indra Nooyi, Kiran Majumdar, Kalpana Chawla, Sania Mirza, Aishwarya Rai and many more have shown to the world that they are no longer a mere housewife.

The Union Cabinet has set a National Policy of Empowerment of Women. It has set the following clear-cut goals and objectives: (i) Creation of an environment through positive economic and social policies for complete development of women in order to make them realize their full potential; (ii) The de-jure and de-facto enjoyment of all human rights and fundamental freedom by women on equal basis with men in all spheres – socio-economic, political, civil and cultural life; (iii) Provide equal access to participation and decision- making of women in social, economic and political life of the country; (iv) seeks the access of women to health care, quality education all levels, career and educational guidance, employment, equal remuneration, occupational health and safety, public office and social security; (v) strengthening legal systems aimed at elimination of all forms of discrimination against women; (vi) changing social attitudes and community practices by active participation and involvement of both men and women; (vii) Elimination of discrimination and all forms in violence against women and the girl child; and building and strengthening partnerships with civil society, particularly women's organisations.

Welfare and development of women constitutes an important part of social welfare and a national plan of action has been formulated for this purpose. The National Committee on women oversees the implementation of policies and programmes for women condensed course of education and vocational training for adult women, hostels for working women, training centres for rehabilitation of destitute women and many other socio-economic programmes for women are being implemented by the governments.

Economic Status of Indian Women

"In my opinion when the history of the last decade comes to be written the palm will be given to the women of India. They have brought Swaraj nearer. They have added several inches to their own height and to that of the nation".

M.K. Gandhi

The contribution of women in economy is fraught with many problem areas. Women have always been working and contributing to the family survival. In a subsistence economy, family being the unit of production and when the major production centre is home, woman's participation in economic activities has been accepted. Among the cultivators, artisans, and those performing manual services in the traditional village economy women have played a distinctive role both in production and marketing. They continue till today wherever the traditional economic forms prevail, particularly among the poor agriculturists, scheduled caste and tribal communities. In the initial phase of industial development, in textiles and jute industries, as well as in mines and plantations women's participation was recognised.

Unfortunately, a good deal of woman's work remains invisible. The contribution of a rural woman working in home, looking after cattle, helping the husband in agricultural work, cooking, bringing fuel and water, goes unrecognised. In case of women in the upper caste and intermediary castes, particularly in the trading and peasant proprietor groups, it is noticed that with the rise of economic status of the family a woman is withdrawn from employment, it is considered a loss of status if she works. But now the situation and value system is different. The people no more think that it is the degradation of their social prestige if their female counterparts working in governmental or non-governmental sectors. The proliferation of administrative jobs both in public and private sector created a demand for educated personnel. Developmental activities and welfare work also made openings for scientific, technical, medical and paramedical persons. Even now-a-days defence sector is opened for girls. Women are attracted for adventurous jobs. But as these women live within the patriarchal, male dominated family structure, a job, however prestigious or lucrative it is, doesn't absolve women from their familial role. Society still considers women's role as primarily home makers.

Economic growth has widened and intensified socio-economic inequalities. Advances in technology have not benefited women. The planned development perspective of the government generated several welfare schemes for bettering women's social and economic position but locked in momentum to empower women and create space to assert as human beings, for about six decades after independence. Women in India have been successful in positively utilizing the benefits provided by the state but not so much as to end the gender discrimination, physical and mental torture, subordinations, marginalisation and trivialisation.

The project and programmes of modernisation which began after India's independence and its concomitant economic empowerment of women have bypassed large majority of women. This was because the planners had no access to details and systematic information about the realities of the lives of ordinary women. Public policy for economic empowerment benefited a large segment of women particularly in states where women were aware which gradually impacted upon the behaviour and attitude of the society towards women and women towards themselves. The development for women and children in rural area (DWCRA) began to work in the second half of the end of the eight plans was introduced in 291 districts. In due course several programmes were introduced like STEP (Support for Employment of Women Programme), grants-in-aid to Mahila Mandals' to encourage women to be self sufficient. Employment Guarantee Scheme (EGS) and the latest is the Mahila Samridhi Yojana (MSY). The national perspective plan for women drawn up as a long term action programme for 1988-2000 has painted out that the core of failure of economic and social empowerment programmes for women was the "half heartedness of implementation".

A major objective of ninth five year plan (1997-2002) was to create an enabling environment where women can freely exercise rights both within and outside home as equal partners of men and the plan document states that this will be realised by early finalisation and adoption of the national policy for the empowerment of women. In the ninth plan, political empowerment is perceived as essential for involving women in the decision making for the realisation of goals envisaged for their social and economic empowerment. The women's movement in India contributed largely for state intervention in the economic sphere, initiate legislation to widen women's entry into education, employment, technology research, management and natural resources and several other socio-economic issues affecting women in the Indian society and polity.

Empowering women with economically productive work will enhance their contribution to agricultural development. Access to resources lays positive impact on them and enhances their decision-making ability to meet some physiological needs like self-esteem and confidence. The Equal Remuneration Act of 1976 provides for payment of equal remuneration for men and women performing the same job. The Factories (Amendment) Act, 1976 provides for compulsory establishment of crèches where at least 30 women are employed.

Political Status of Indian Women

Political participation of women refers to a process of "authoritative allocation of values in a society". All kinds and all levels of activity-voting, contesting in elections, campaigning, party activism, pressure group membership and extra-institutional or agitational activity of any kind at informal level aimed at influencing the policy makers and ministerial office are subsumed to construct the profile of political participation of women in India.

Democracy presupposes equality of all and also equality of opportunity to all as to participation in the decision making process in public bodies including all governmental and representative institutions irrespective of differences in castes, creed, language, religion, sex or place of birth.

Political participation of Indian women started with the freedom movement. Mahatma Gandhi was very much instrumental for arousing political consciousness in the poor, illiterate women and making them take part in the freedom movement. Political participation may be defined as voluntary participation in political affairs through membership, voting and partaking in the activities of the political parties and legislative bodies. The constitution of India guarantees adult franchise and provides the framework for women to participate actively in politics.

The Indian constitution asserts the equality of sexes and prohibits discrimination solely on the ground of sex. It also guarantees universal adult franchise and provides the framework for women to participate actively in politics. Article 15 of the constitution prohibits discrimination on the grounds of religion, race, caste, sex or place of birth. It is a pity that women have not substantially availed of the constitutional provisions. The successive election statistics shows that the number of women who exercise their franchise has increased from election to election. For the last two decades almost equal numbers of men and women have gone to the polling booths to vote.

The number of women filing their nomination papers in any election, national or state, is only a fraction at the last moment and the contesting candidates become fewer in number. Ultimately the number of women winning elections will be so small that their percentage in the legislative body will be nominal.

Table 8.2

Women Members in Lok Sabha

Lok Sabha	*Year*	*Total No. of Seats*	*Total No. of Women*	*Percentage*
First	1952-57	499	22	4.4
Second	1957-62	500	27	5.4
Third	1962-67	503	34	6.7
Fourth	1967-71	523	31	5.9
Fifth	1971-76	521	22	4.8
Sixth	1977-80	544	19	3.4
Seventh	1980-84	544	28	5.1
Eighth	1984-89	544	44	8.1
Ninth	1989-91	529	28	5.3
Tenth	1991-96	509	36	7.1
Eleventh	1996-98	537	34	6.3
Twelfth	1998-99	543		
Thirteenth	1999-04	543	42	7.8

The percentage of winning candidates has been below ten in parliament, in all the past elections, as shown in the chart. The state assemblies too present a similar situation. In the same period, Indian women have achieved commendable progress in literacy, education, and employment. They have achieved rights equal to that of men for parental assets.

The concept of empowerment is related to women's powerlessness rather than the issue of development. Women's powerlessness and non-participation in political affairs arise from their illiteracy, lack of awareness, information, knowledge about markets, skill, esteem, money, job opportunities, self-confidence and so on. Monkman's strategies for women's empowerment are: (1) Integrated development; (2) Economic development; and (3) consciousness raising. Her integrated approach specifies poverty, lower access to health care, education etc. as the reasons of women's powerlessness. Consciousness can be raised by understanding the complexities of gender relations and women's status, a broader understanding of male dominance, discrimination and enable women to formulate their strategy.

Women are excluded from participation in public affairs because of the presumption that they lack in leadership skills. Traditionally qualities of leadership are identified as masculine. Women are supposed to be compassionate, emotional, mild, submissive and therefore relegated to the margin as unfits in political leadership. Women leaders are expected to maintain a balance between family and their workplace even when they are assigned high leadership responsibilities. This expectation is not with male leaders as they are free from sharing domestic work.

Even though the constitutions of most of the independent states have incorporated equal rights for men and women in principle; it is never in practice except in voting as most of the political parties bank upon women voters. Hence there are not many women in politics it is obvious that they are invisible in decision making and in ensuring implementation of the decisions. Political parties include agenda for women's development promising a certain percentage of sets but never show their keenness in getting the quota achieved particularly in high level decision making institutions as has been the experience with the proposed Women's Reservation Bill (Lok Sabha in India).

The system of reserving for women 33 per cent seats in parliament already exists in Russia, the Philippines, Korea etc. In certain other countries—Norway, Sweden, France, Germany, etc. — the political parties take initiative to reserve 33 per cent seats for women. Both ways it has worked well. Unfortunately in India, no political party has come forward with the suggestion of reserving the candidature for women. It seems impossible on the part of political parties arriving at a consensus on the issue is remote.

The male dominated political parties are interested only in the female vote bank. They are not interested to promote female membership in the party beyond a certain limit so that men could hold maximum number of important positions. Reservation of seats for women in panchayats to parliament is a small step to realise the women's rising aspirations and much more remains to be achieved if women will have to play a significant role in decision making.

Conclusion

Nature has made men and women differently in their bodies and their mental make-up. Therefore some of their problems are different. Women suffer from some disabilities which are absent in the case of men. A woman has to be educated, beautiful and submissive. This is the view of a husband. It is not possible to change the condition of women through law and legislation. After all legislation is only on instrument. But, until the women get rid of their mental slavery, regain their self-confidence, get over fear of society and overcome superstitions, they can't aspire for freedom.

In conclusion, it can be said that women are not generally treated well in family and society. The main reason for their ill-treatment and backwardness is that the majority of the girls and women have no access to education. The position and education of Scheduled Tribe women is still lower. At the lower level, the word exploitation, both mental and physical, is the watch word. Though the impact of science and technology is visible in every sphere of life, the women have not really benefited from them. Media has an important role to play in upgrading the position of women in society. Voluntary organisations have been championing the cause of women in the past and they are expected to do so in future also. For the proper development of women in terms of socio-economic and political point of view, their mental health is also an important factor. Finally, the establishment of women's commission and rational women's information centre was felt necessary for the integrated development of women.

9

ORISSA WOMEN IN POLITICS

MAMATA KUMARI SUAR*

Introduction

A study of the political participation of women in a state like Orissa is a difficult task for a verity of reasons. Women in Orissa like the other Indian women began their national life with certain handicaps. In the pre-independent India, Orissa was a mixed bag of princely states having separate administrative system. Because of the continuation of feudal role in these states and late exposure to the west, general progress and political awakening in all fields were rather slow compared to the rest of the country. The subordination of women by way of domesticity and lack of freedom of movement, lack of education and economic unbalance, that resulted low quality of life for women. All these reasons provide explanation for the fact of political inactivity of women in Orissa. In addition, this had prevented women from contributing to the freedom struggle of the country.

The present paper studies the women in politics, a case study. It seeks to deal with participation and voting behaviour of women. Political participation has been divided into two categories:

* Research Scholar, Berhampur University, Orissa.

1. Involvement in Politics; and
2. Contesting in elections.

Women politics is the most important factor. The debate was at the center stage in the international arena in 1994 UN Conference in Cairo, UNI's fourth International Conference on Women at Beijing in 1995 and UNOs Social Summit Conference at Copenhagen in March 1995. The UN International Conference on Population and Development (ICPD) 1994 in its guiding principles states that the human rights of women and girl child are an inalienable, integral and indivisible part of universal human rights. The full and equal participation of women in civil, cultural, economic, political and social life at the national, regional and international levels and the eradication of all forms of discrimination on grounds of sex are primary objectives of international community. Indian women continue to languish in a patriarchal society and a colossal percentage of them largely belonging to traditional and religious orthodox families deprived of social mobility and enjoy low social status.

The Government of India has taken numerous measures and has made honest endeavours to raise the status of women and establish gender equality. The constitutional obligations as well as different plans, programmes and policies have laid emphasis in women empowerment in order to bring them to the mainstream of development.

Article 15 of the Constitution prohibits any discrimination on the grounds of sex, while Article 15(3) clarifies that this provision will not prevent the state from making any special provision for women.

Article 42 of the Constitution envisages that the state shall make provision for securing just and humane conditions of work and maternity relief. Besides the directive principles of state policy, also urge that the state shall direct its policy towards securing adequate livelihood for women and ensuring equal pay for equal work for both men and women.

The Eighth-Five-Year Plan intends at enabling women to function as equal partners and participations in development by extending the services to women both qualitatively and quantitatively. In addition, another plan is legislation for women by formulating and strengthening grass root level women's grasp.

The highly literate women and women belonging to socially, economically and politically advanced upper strata of urban society are largely enjoying the fruits of women welfare measures. Colossal large percentages of women are engaged in the unpaid household activities and are largely employed in informal and unorganized private sector. Only 14.1 per cent women are employed in organised sector and they earn less than their male counterparts of the society. Due to domination of patriarchy norm most of the women do not enjoy property rights. Since independence, there is some improvement of female literacy. The male literacy before independence was 25 per cent after independence, it increased from 7.9 per cent to 39.29 per cent, and the literacy status on rural and SC and ST women are very negligible in comparison to urban women.

Women Politics in Pre-independence Period

Women inOrissa are shy in nature and they do not take part in politics because they are conservative in nature. Political participation by them started during the Indian freedom struggle. Gandhiji in particular was conscious of the role of women in the freedom struggle. The women struggled against a powerful obstinate colonial regime because of their courage, endurance and moral strength. Gandhi's call to women-folk, his identification of women's self-image, development with the cause of nationalist movement and a reformed socio-political order helped in mobilising the vast multitude of women. Thus, women in Orissa have their first socialisation in the political sphere during the struggle for independence. Orissa women availed greater opportunities to participate in the reconstruction of society and legislative politics after Orissa became a separate state in 1936 within British administrations. Our independence movement produced some eminent women leaders like Annie Besant, Sarojini Naidu and Durga Bai. Rapid expansion of communication, education, industrialisation and urbanisation brought about some changes in the attitude and outlook of Indian women. To some extent, women became interested to participate in politics by the spread of literacy and mass communication.

Some prominent women of the state took part in India's freedom struggle; they were Malati Choudhury, Rama Devi, Sarala Devi and Arnapurna Maharana. The women fighters, who took part in the Salt Agitation in 1936, had also joined in the Quit India Movement of 1942 and they were put behind the bars several times. Some of them had also joined in the Prajamandal Movement. At that time, the numbers of women freedom fighters were very small. These women came only from the middle class families whose male members themselves were active participants in freedom struggle. Scheduled caste and scheduled tribe women were a few among the female freedom fighters.

In the second part of the 19th century and in the early phase of 20th century, a few tribal women led the revolt in Koraput district against British rule. Bangara Devi, a Koya princess who ascended the throne of Malkangiri in 1835 attacked British troops in 1860 and Khare Prava a Banda women objected to the British rule. Another tribal woman who took part in the anti-British movement was Laxmi Saurani, a Saura by caste, who belonged to a small village near Gunupur. She was an active volunteer.

Women are Negligible Participants in Politics Because of Inadequate Representation

Until today, women representations are not adequately in the legislature, executive and judiciary of the country. It could be remarked that although the recent years witnessed an increase in women voters, participation has not been accompanied by changes in similar magnitude in the number of women occupying decision-making positions. In India, women's representation in Parliament and in the State Assembly has never gone beyond 8 and 10 per cent respectively. In recent years due to reservation of seats, there has been increased participation of grass root democratic system. Despite women's political empowerment at the grass root democracy a colossal large percentage of them is acting as de jure pradhans and panchayat members under the shadow of the husband-in-laws and parents. Not only in legislative sphere but also in the executive and in judiciary spheres women are thinly represented. A meager percentage of women are positioned in Indian Administrative Service (IAS), Indian Police Service (IPS) and Allied Services. As representation of women in judiciary is concerned, Supreme Court and High Courts have history of fewer number of women judges.

In the social sphere, there is "gender isolation" and "gender oppression". The UNFPA reports on the state of world population—1997 envisages that there has been increase violence against women in the past decade in India. In the traditionally and religiously orthodox societies, women are not allowed to formulate Mahila Mandal and they silently bear the atrocities and became victim of 'wife beating', 'bride burning' molestation, rape and other types of physical and socio-psychological harassment. Being isolated from special sphere women are less represented in sports and business because of gender stereotypes. In equal terms, women are also less involved in trade unions and labour associations. A society that has effectively implemented women welfare measures, has ensured gender Justice and empowerment of women, has achieved greater social development. In India Kerala is an outstanding example of society-advanced state and Bihar is one of the socially backward states. Women are the vital human infrastructure and their empowerment economic, educational, social and political would hasten the peace of social development. Investing in women's capabilities and empowering them to achieve their choices and opportunities is the surest way to political growth and over all development.

A glance at the following table reveals the trend of women's development.

Table 9.1

Sl. No.	*Women empowerment indicators*	*Socially development State Kerala*	*Socially backward State Bihar*	*All India*
1.	Women literacy	86.20	20.90	39.30
2.	Sex ratio	1068	956	927
3.	Percentage of women voting in Parliament	72.59	47.89	55

Objective of the Study

The objective of the study is to focus the socio-economic background and political participation of women in Panchayat Raj Institutions. So far, no study has highlighted on political participation of women in this reason the area is specifically important because it has a rural social-economic structure and traditional culture. In such a situation, women have scanty freedom to participate in public activities. Therefore, the present study aims to explore the nature of political participation of women in this rural set up. In the present study, we have dealt with the nature of participation of women in politics. For this we have also make use of mandate the representation of women in Parliament as well as in the Orissa Legislative Assembly.

In order to get a comparative picture of women's political participation before independence and after it, we have studied the role of Oriya women in freedom struggle and their representation in Orissa Legislature:

Review of Literacy

Realising the importance of socio-political and economic environment of women, the present study attracted the attention of academicians and research institutions.

Veena Pooncha's "Understanding Women's Studies" seeks to explain the socio-historical, cultural, economic and political reasons for women's subordination. The book examines how women's studies alter the theories and methods of social sciences. It also discusses the theoretical under premising of women's studies and its concepts.

Kamala Bhasin's "What is Patriarchy" discussed about the meaning, nature, origin and roots of patriarchy in question and answer style. J.K. Baral and B.B. Jena's "Orissa Government and Politics" clears the role of women in Orissa Government before independence and after independence.

M.K. Gandhi in his "Social Justice" states the rights of Oriya women in Indian and Orissan. Sudhakar Patnaik's 'History of Freedom Movement' in Orissa analyses the leadership and cooperation of Oriya women during pre-independence period and at the time of freedom movement.

Giri Raj Gupta's "Family and Social Change" in Modern India describes the modernisation and participation of women in the culture of Orissa and India. The progress of the country and state depends on development of women in socio-political and economically sphere. B.L. Fadia's "Indian Government and Politics" provides constitutional rights and reservation of women in India's political system.

Another feminist scholar whose work is very useful in understanding patriarchy is Gendalerner. In the book "the Creation of Patriarchy", she has argued against struggle cause theories and against looking for the historical moment when patriarch was established. She explains the importance of women's history in women's struggle against patriarch and for equality.

Sylvia Walby in her book "Theorising Patriarchy" calls patriarchy as a system of social structures and practices in which men dominate oppress and exploit women.

Heidi Huntsman's "The unhappy marriage of Marxism and Feminism" towards a more progressive union" is to discuss a very close line between patriarchy and capitalism. She argues that patriarchy has a material basis. The material base upon which patriarchy, rests lies nest, fundamentally in men's control over women's labour.

Kalyani Menon Sen and A.K. Siva Kumar's book "Women in India: How Free? How Equal" is an independent, analytical report commissioned by the UN system? This is among the first UNDAF initiatives of the UN family. This report is a small effort to bring issues of women's freedom and gender equality more centrally into the arena of public debate and to make these the concerns of every citizen.

From the present study, sources of secondary data have immensely helpful to me. All the available literatures are collected from different sources to get my self-acquainted with this selected study.

Methodology

The present study is descriptive in nature. It keeps a record of secondary data, published and unpublished journals, newspapers, and research articles and books and booklets materials relating to the study.

Sampling

Because of limited time at our disposal as well as the paucity of resources, it was not possible to make our study geographically representative of the whole of Orissa.

Key Research Questions

Women have long been a suppressed group and they are discriminated by male counterparts of the society. Men in most advanced countries dominate the women also. This practice can be changed by women's liberation movements, which have started from western countries. Development of a country is correlated with the status of women in that country. A corollary of this hypothesis is that the nature of women's participation in politics is greatly affected by the development of a country. Further, the socio-economic status of a woman tends to affect her political participation.

Limitations of the Study

The study is limited to selected villages of a block. Being a case study, the findings of the studies may not be universally appreciable. Besides, there are some developed and underdeveloped villages in the block. In this study an intensive investigation has been conducted on selected villages of the underdeveloped areas. Therefore, the findings refer to this area. It might be similar in underdeveloped regions but for its universal applicability, further extensive and intensive exploration will be required. Despite limitations, the findings might bring into force several aspects of rural society related to political participation.

Hypotheses

It is proposed to examine the following hypotheses in the present study:

1. The political awareness of women in general is law;
2. Women are politically less active than their male counterparts of the society;
3. The women of the upper strata of the society are politically more advanced than those of lower strata;

4. Young generation is more advanced than the old generation in consideration of political awareness;
5. Political awareness and political efficacy of women are correlated with their political participation;
6. In case of social perception the young women are more advanced than the old women.

Political Participation of Women in Orissa and India

The place of women in any country is linked with the society in which they live. Since the inception of humankind women have formed an inseparable part of society and culture , not only in the demographic sense where women continue to come close to men in numbers, but even in the area of social organisation and pattern of culture, women's place cannot be undermined. This fact is true irrespective of the type of society *viz.* traditional, transitional and so-called modern ones. Almost all societies in time and space have demarcated for various purposes, the world of men and the world women.

The Indian democracy inaugurated in 1950 with a written Constitution have guaranteed to all women fundamental rights and equal political participation. It recognises the political rights of women without any discrimination, to participate in all national level decision making.

In India, women constitute half of the population. However, they are neglected and backward class. They are social beings. First, we should know about their socio-economic and political position in our society. Socio-economic and political indictors are not sufficient to explain their position in the society because women irrespective of class, caste and race are under the boundary of male dominance.

Home caring and child rearing is almost obligatory for all women in the society. In rural areas, it is their assigned and compulsory job to bring fuel, fodder, water and to cook. This ultimately makes women's surrounding completely narrow. Here it lays the importance for discussion about the gender development programmes and their empowerment.

In productive field, women are marginalised mainly in the unorganised sector because of their lower proficiency and are paid lower wages. In the sphere of family management, they work hard and take full care of their children and family members. This service is considered as the natural extension of their role as mother and are not given due weightage. Men being the bread earner of the family remain the absolute decision maker.

This pattern of gender relationship extends to the political sphere also except in few countries. Now-a-day's men and women enjoy legally, equal political status. This does not mean automatic enjoyment of the rights. Rights conferred on women in rural perspective show that women are still second-class citizens. In every society virtually men enjoys the higher ranks of power. Despite the prominence of a few women who have gained high political positions in a few countries such as India, Pakistan, Bangaladesh and Srilanka, Israel, Great Britain are lesser status enjoyed by women. Discrimination on the grounds of sex is not only undemocratic but also immoral and illegal. However, gender equality can come out only when women make use of the full anjoy of political weapons available to them to achieve it. Political activity is essential to the struggle for women's liberation.

In India, there has been legal and constitutional status of women from the very beginning of independence. This guarantee of equal rights, conferred on women has empowered them to participate in the democratic political process of the country. According to the report from UNI, female electorates are higher in number than the male counterpart. In 1991 General Election, in India 24,38,70,209 women exercised their franchise. The next five years saw an increase of about 15 per cent on the other hand. The male voters in 1991 were 27,02,56,181, which increased 13.5 per cent in 1995. An interesting trend was found in the growth of women voters in Nagaland. From 1991 to 1996, they registered a 15.96 per cent increase, while the growth rate of male voters was only 0.51 per cent. This report indicates that women participation is higher in franchise system.

Before India's independence, Orissa had provincial elections for two legislative assemblies in 1936 and 1946. Only 3.3 per cent of assembly members were women in these assemblies. Since the first General Election of free India, the physical participation of women has increased from 4 to 42 in the 10th assembly election. It has increased by 10.5 times within a span of four decade. In the first election to the state legislature 3 out of 4 women contestants were elected but the result was proper in subsequent elections. In eighth assembly state election 1 out of 42 women got elected. In the sixth assembly election in 1985, the highest number of women got elected. Though in terms of percentage, it is not the highest. This indicates the disprortionate rate between male and female represented in the Assembly.

The following table provides a clear picture of participation of women in election to the Orissa Legislative Assembly in different elections.

Table 9.2

Participation of women in the elections to the Orissa Legislative Assembly (1952-1990)

Year	*Contested*		*Elected*		*Total Contested*	*Total Elected*
	Male	*Female*	*Male*	*Female*		
1952	433	04	137	03	437	140
1957	493	15	135	05	508	140
1961	523	10	136	04	533	140
1967	591	12	136	04	603	140
1971	823	12	140	00	835	140
1974	707	15	142	04	722	146
1977	587	17	140	07	604	147
1980	720	16	142	05	736	147
1985	768	25	139	08	793	147
1990	871	42	140	07	913	147

The proceeding table reveals that elections to the 10th Orissa Legislative Assembly held on 27 February 1990 has its significance for the first time in the state electoral history because the maximum number (1/2) of women contested in the state election. It speaks for the fact of growing consciousness and increasing participation of Oriya women in the electoral politics. The increasing number of women contestants in the recent election indicates that national parties in Orissa are putting up more women candidates compared to the past election. In order to give representation to all sections of the society in the legislative body, our constitution has ensured adequate representation to scheduled caste and scheduled tribe through reservation of seats in these bodies. Despite these provisions, the state of Orissa failed to put up any SC/ST women in the state legislature and Parliament till 1980. The observation reveals that four tribal women in 1980 elections and five tribal women from Western Orissa in 1985 elections got elected to the Assembly. In the 2000 election no tribal women have succeeded to the floors of Vidhan Sabha, though a considerable number of tribal women contested in the elections. In the present assembly election, only SC women named Pramila Mallick has became the winner.

It is interesting to observe that Western Orissa accounts for more number of women contestants than Eastern Orissa, Mayurbhanj accounts for two women contestants and Koraput accounts for six women contestants. An increasing number of tribal women contestants in the election speaks for the fact that why Western Orissa accounts for more number of women contestants.

Women's Representation in the Parliament from 1952-2005

The data on representation of Oriya women in the national parliament show a dismal picture. Until 1980, no women contestant was elected to the Lok Sabha. The situation changed with the election of Ms. Jayanti Patnaik, wife of Mr. J.B. Patnaik one of the Chief Minister of the state to the Lok Sabha in the by-election held in 1981.

Women in Ministries

A poor representation of women has been noticed in the composition of all ministries since Orissa achieved statehood in April 1936. Due to political instability, the state has witnessed more than necessary elections and thereby a number of ministries. Yet five women have become ministers; they are: Ms. Basant Manjari Devi, Ms. Saraswati Pradhan, Ms. Saraswati Hembrum, Ms. Frida Tapno and Ms. Nandini Satpathy, who became the Chief Minister of the state. The Biju Patnaik ministry in 1961 had no women member. In 1959, Kanaka Lata Deo was elected as the first and so far only women Speaker of the House. Another significant feature in the 10th Assembly is that four out of seven MLAs belong to royal families; they are Ms. Santi Devi, Ms. Srushree Devi, Sugyani Kumari Deo and Usha Devi.

Poor representation of women in the state legislature and union parliament accounted for such small number of women in the ministries.

The trend of male domination of political parties that selected candidates is also responsible for such a state of affair. It reveals that although quite a few political parties have participated in the elections. Majority of the women contestants were from Indian National Congress 57 out of 177 women that contested since 1936 until today in different elections to state legislative assembly and parliament belong to congress party.

Table 9.3

Women members in Lok Sabha

Year	*Total number*	*Total contestant*	*Total women contestant*	*No. of women members elected*	*Percentage of total seats*
1952	499	1864	51	22	4.4
1951	500	1591	70	27	5.4
1962	503	1985	68	34	6.7
1967	523	2396	66	31	5.9
1971	521	2784	86	22	4.2
1977	544	2439	70	19	3.4
1980	544	4620	142	28	7.9
1984	544	5481	159	44	8.1
1989	517	6160	185	27	5.3
1991	544	8699	325	39	7.16
1996	543	14214	491	39	7.18

Table 9.4

Women members in Rajya Sabha

Year	*Total number*	*Total women members*	*Percentage of total seats*
1952	219	16	7.3
1957	237	18	7.5
1962	238	18	7.5
1967	240	20	8.3
1971	243	17	7.0
1977	244	25	10.2
1980	244	24	9.8
1985	244	28	11.4
1990	245	24	9.7
1991	245	38	15.5

Table 9.5

Women MLAs profile (1952 to 1980)

Year	*No. of Candidates*	*Women Candidates*	*Total Seats*	*Elected Women Candidates*
1952	517	04	140	03
1957	508	16	140	05
1961	533	10	140	01
1967	603	12	140	05
1971	835	12	140	00
1974	722	15	147	04
1977	603	18	147	07
1980	781	16	147	05

Between 1952 and 1980, only a small number of women have been elected to the Orissa Legislative Assembly while in 1952 there were only 3 women MLAs in 1980 election. Five women MLAs were elected. But it is not significant improvement. Because as early as in 1957 there were five women MLAs elected. In 1971 there were no single women elected. In 1977, seven women were elected as MLAs.

Role of Women in National Politics

Almost every argument for and against the women's reservation bill has been said and heard. Then how did women's reservation in Panchayats and Nagar Palikas find approval from the same patriarchs' politics that now prevents their entry in Parliament.

Clearly postcolonial states like India have to become stronger and more mature before they can deliver social and gender justice. Difficulty as it was for women to swallow, it also legitimised the idea that women's rights could be defined by the religion on community they belong to. New alliances like the National Federation of Dalit Women (NFDW) and the National Alliance of Women Organisation (NAWO) have much to do in mobilising women from all over the country to articulate their issues, concerns, hopes and visions for an egalitarian society. Both organisations have started with vigour and NAWO has to its credit the drafting of country's first women's political manifesto in 1996 to challenge all political parties before the general elections that year. Both the groups have proven potential to redefine complex issues.

Profile of Women Leaders

In the post-independence period, many Oriya women have been elected as MLAs and MPs and participated in the political life of the state. It is however; worth nothing, that many women who were active during the freedom struggle did not try to become MLAs and MPs. Of course, Malati Choudhury contested unsuccessfully in Dhenkanal constituency. During those days when a women coming out from the household was against social decorum. These women had taken tremendous risks and made great sacrifices by jumping into the independence movement with their counterpart male freedom fighters. After India won, independence women entered elective politics and became a part of a power structure. In case of male politicians, participation in the freedom struggle, so to say, became a sort of profitable investment. However, the women freedom fighters largely, set a glorious example by abstaining from power politics in the post-independence period. They virtually proved that their participation in the freedom movement was pure, noble and without any personal motive.

On the other hand, those women who were later elected as MLAs and MPs had little to do with the independence movement. Further most of these women leaders both freedom fighters and power seekers belonging to upper stratum of the society. Hardly has any woman from the lower rung of the society even been elected either to the Orissa Legislative Assembly or to the Parliament accepting the reserve quota candidates. Thus, there is a linkage between one's socio-economic status and political recruitment and participation. Further, some women belonging to families of ex-rulers (Raja and Zamindars) have become MLAs and MPs. It shows that "royal" connection helps to women in becoming MLAs and MPs. The validity of these general propositions is known from the profiles of women elites of Orissa drawn below.

Rama Devi

Rama Devi was born in affluent family. However, she has always been drawn towards the poor. It has been her mission in life to serve the poor. Her father was Gopal Ballav Das whose elder brother was Madhusudan Das, popularly known as "Madhu Babu" in Orissa. Madhu Babu the creator of modern Orissa in 1936 was an ideal for Rama Devi. She did not have any formal schooling, but was educated at home. Politics was not her choice. But she took active role in the movement for creation of Orissa as an autonomous state. She was imprisoned in 1930 for this. She married to Gapabandhu Choudhury who was the Congress leader at that time and he was joined in the freedom movement.

After the conclusion of the Gandhi – Irwin Pact in1931, Rama Devi jumped into the national activities and joined the march (Padayatra of Harijans). From 1932 onwards she became directly involved in the freedom movement of India. Though not a member of any organisation yet, she was an inseparable part of all the organisations like Kasturba Trust, Gandhi Trust, Harijan Organisations, Khadi work and Sarvodaya Mandal. Having been involved in all the revolutionary events of national importance, she herself was an inspiration to others. Keeping the movement ablaze, Rama Devi was again jailed during the August Revolution in 1942. Her participation in the August Revolution prompted her to organise the womenfolks through her speeches in various congregations.

Though Rama Devi had no desire for direct politics, she was forced to be involved indirectly only for the common course. She was neither an office bearer nor a member of any political organisation or interest group. Being influenced by Gandhiji, she took the lead in the agitation of Harijans, from 1932 to 1934. She was the Chairman of the Harijan Seva Sangha. During the Salt Movement, along with others she directly violated the British laws at Inchudi of Balasore district and at Kujanga in Cuttack district. For this she was taken into the police custody. Rama Devi was not in the forefront of the Praja Mandal Movement. But she moved from village to village in some Garjats along with Malati Choudhury to inspire the people to fight for their freedom.

Now India is an independent country. However, those who are dedicated workers and patriots have withdrawn themselves from the national politics after the Gandhian light was extinguished. Being unhappy with the "check and kill intrigue" on the chessboard of both national and provincial politics, Rama Devi has confined herself only to the service of the depressed and the downtrodden community.

Sarala Devi

Sarala Devi was one of the foremost women leaders in Orissa to have fought not only for the creation of Orissa as a separate state but also for the independence of India. She was inspired a great deed by her husband, Bhagirathi Mahapatra who himself was a freedom fighter. In 1930 when the civil disobedience was launched, she was working in Ganjam at that time a part of Madras presidency, for the cause of Orissa autonomy. She counted her days in jail along with many other women leaders from different parts of the country; prominent among them was Durgabai Deshmukh. After the Gandhi–Irwin Pact of 1931, Sarala Devi was again imprisoned as she joined the Salt Movement under the inspiring leadership of Madhu Babu. Sarala Devi vigorously worked for the creation of Orissa as a separate state; she was not very active in the praja mandal movement launched against the tyranny of exalters. But through her emotional speeches, she was able to raise the people and voices their grievances against their ruler. She of course was not jailed in 1942. But she was an active participant in August revolution of that year.

After Orissa was made a separate state in 1936, Sarala Devi was elected to Orissa Legislative Assembly. She raised her voice against social injustice, blind believe and social dogmas. After independence was achieved, she remained aloof from active politics. However, through her subtle political comments, she has been able to influence the public opinion in the state. Of late, her first love has been literary activities rather than politics.

Malati Choudhury

In 1905, Malati Devi was born in a humble middle class family in Calcutta. Her father and mother were Kumud Nath Sen, Snehalata Sen. Her two brothers were Kulprasad Sen, and Pradyat Kumar Sen. It is the influence of her ideal parents that shaped the life of Malati Sen. In 1921 when Malati tried to keep away from the HSC Examination her elder brother Kulprasad convinced her to appear at the examination. Thereafter she entered Shantiniketan for higher studies. She went through a large number of Tagore's writings, which left a lasting mark in her mind. Many times, she left the college campus in response to Gandhiji's call for non-cooperation movement. She was strongly attached towards the freedom struggle. Malati Devi's involvement in the independence movement was intensified after her marriage with Nabakrushna Choudhury, an Oriya youth dedicated to the cause of Indian freedom. They formed a perfect combination. Being inspired by her husband, Malati Devi neglected the worldly pleasures and dedicated herself to the greater cause of the nation.

She took active part in the salt movement launched at Inchudi of Balasore district and Kujanga of Cuttack district. For her criticism of British policies, the police often harassed her. Though the role of women in making Orissa a separate state was not significant, yet their contribution in this regard cannot be ignored. Though born and brought up in Bengal, Malati Devi still favoured a separate political identity for Orissa. Her Bengali background did not prevent her from raising her voice in favour of the movement for the creation of a separate Orissa state.

On 1 April 1936, Orissa became a separate state. But the rulers of different princely states joined hands with the British government in frustrating the efforts to merge them with Orissa.

In exchange of police help from the British government, they connived with it to kill the nationalist movement. This give rise to popular revolt in ex-princely states against the native rulers. The people's movement became intense between 1936 and 1938. Malati Devi was the first female leader in Orissa to have jumped into the movement at different areas like Talcher, Dhenkanal, Nayagarh and Nilgir. She strongly opposed the police repression and influenced the people by delivering a hard-hitting speech against the kings in a public meeting held at Jenapur in 1938. She exhorted all the farmers to revolt against the Zamindars and moved in person from village to village speaking against feudalism and appealing people not give any gift or share to the landowners.

Malati Devi formed a farmer's organisation and became its joint secretary. Under her leadership the farmer's agitation in Madhupur, Kujanga and Sukinda became strikingly noteworthy. In the meantime a socialist party was formed in the Congress. Along with her husband Malati Devi worked hard for the socialist movement at the cost of their home and comforts. She was a devoted follower of Gandhiji. She was always in the forefront wherever Gandhiji called for direct action against the Britishers. Taking active part in the Quit India Movement she courted Jail in 1942. Besides she tried her best to serve the public when she was on tour to Nuakhai with Gandhiji. She had the courage to visit the area infested by bitter communication, which raised its ugly need on the narrow of independence.

Malati Devi was the only women from Orissa who was elected to the constituent assembly in 1946. Though a signatory to the constitution, she left the constituent assembly in order to shun the unwanted arrogance of big leaders. Hence her political involvement was not confined to a narrow provincial plane. Rather she was thrown into national current of action.

In 1946 when H.K. Mahtab was the Chief Minister of Orissa, Malati Devi became the President of the Provincial Congress Committee by defeating Biswanath Das, an Ex-Prime Minister of Orissa. She opposed some of the government proposals even when she was the president of the Congress party. It shows that she was a democrat and strong fighter of good causes. Party constants would not defer her from fighting for noble causes.

Between 1946 and 1948 the people movement was again intensified in different princely states with the demand for the merger of these states with Orissa. Malati Devi who initially was in the forefront of the people's movement returned to her old battlefield to provide leadership. The merger except Mayurbhanj was accomplished in 1948. The latter was merged next year.

Malati Devi had right connections and right background, which she could have profitably cashed in. But she did not do that. She devoted her life to the service of the poor, depressed and downtrodden in the society. In Orissa she is one of the important lights of the Sarvodaya Movement. A life long fighter against corruption and injustice, she joined the total revolution of Jaya Prakash Narayan, Orissa is proud of her who has been a temple of service to the nation.

Annapurna Maharana

The true daughter of a true mother, Annapurna was largely influenced by her maternal grand-father, Gopal Ballav Das, from her early days and was also greatly influence by her illustrious parents, namely Gopabandhu Choudhury and Rama Devi. She had so much hatred for Britishers that she did not attend any school because all the educational institutions were controlled by the Britishers those days. Being persuaded by her parents she agreed to get her early education at home like her parents and brother Manamohan Choudhury. She prefered to sacrifice worldly comforts for the service of the nation. In 1932 and 1942, along with her mother, she was imprisoned due to her deep involvement in the freedom struggle. She never contested any election. She was active in the Sarvodaya Movement. She was dissatisfied with the present political system. She believed that women participation in politics may help in curing this diseased system.

Subhadra Mahatab

Subhadra Mahatab, wife of Dr. H.K. Mahatab extended solid support to her husband in his struggle for national independence. For her active involvement in the freedom struggle she was taken into custody twice. She capably managed the Gandhi Karnabandi founded by Mahatab at Agar Pada, her native place in Balasore District. She was a devoted disciple of Gandhiji. She was associated with several socio-cultural institutions like Gapabandhu

Choudhury Ashram at Bani and Jivaraj Kalyanji Ashram near Bhadrak. Gandhiji visited the latter in 1934 and praised Subhadra Devi as a good lady who was familiar with spinning. She donated all her golden ornaments to Gandhiji for the welfare of Harijans. In 1967 she was elected to the Orissa Legislative Assembly from Bhubaneswar constituency in a by-elections.

Basanta Manjari Devi

Basanta Manjari Devi was the "Queen Mother" of Ranpur which became famous for the Praja Mandal Movement that led to the death of political agent Bazelgettle. Like all other ex-rulers, the ruler of Ranpur was pro-British and obviously opposed to the Congress party, which fought for India's independence. Soon after independence, Basanta Manjari Devi joined the Congress party and became one of its important creams of the crop. In 1952, she was elected to the Orissa Legislative Assembly on Congress ticket from Ranapur and was made a deputy minister. In 1951, she was re-elected to the assembly from the same constituency as a Congress candidate and was elected to the cabinet rank. She was a good social worker. Her lasting contribution to the state and nation is the TB Hospital at Chandpur. It is biggest of the kind in Asia. Hundreds of TB patients has been cured every year.

Ratna Prava Devi

Ratna Prava Devi was the wife of late Raja Pratap Singh Deo, Mihindra Bahadur of Dhenkanal. She was the daughter of Maharaja Sri Adhitya Pratap Singh Deo of Sarerkalla, which is now a part of Jharkhands. Born in 1909, Ratna Prava was active in scouts' movement and as a state commissioner of Girls Guides; she represented India in Kensington Geri scout function held in 1937. During the Darbar administration, she was in charge of public health, women education and endowment development. First, she was the district President of the Ganatantra Party. Then she continued as the district president when the party merged with the Swatantana in 1936. Ratna Prava Devi was elected to the Orissa Legislative Assembly in 1951, 1961 and 1967. She took a lot of interest in the education and health of her constituency. She was a member of the Utkal University Senate, State National Saving Advisory Board and an executive member of the state bench of Red Cross Society.

Nandini Satpathy

Politics and literature rarely combine. Nevertheless, they did on Mrs. Nandini Satpathy. The Ex-Chief Minister of Orissa, daughter of an eminent writer, Kalindi Charan Panigrahi who belonged to Purim District. Nandini got married to Debendra Satpathy who belongs to Dhenkanal District. As a student leader, Nandini made a name in 1950s, when women politics was almost an unthinkable. She had the courage and determination to be an activist and during her student days at Revenshaw College, Cuttack, she emerged as a courageous women activist who did not admit that sex was a barrier to doing active politics. She was greatly influenced by late Bhagabati Panigrahi, her father's brother who was not only a great progressive writer, but also one of the founding factors of the Communist Party in Orissa. No wonder since her childhood, Nandini was attracted towards communism. She became active in student politics and was an important functionary of the All India Students Federation, the Students' wing of the CPI.

Nandini switched over to the Congress Party in early 1960's. In 1962, she was elected to the Rajya Sabha and was re-elected in 1968. In a short span time, she made her presence felt at New Delhi and was able to win the confidence of Indira Gandhi, the Prime Minister. First, she was appointed as a Deputy Minister. Quickly she was promoted to the rank of state Minister-in-Charge of Communication and Broadcasting. In 1972, she returned to the state politics. She was appointed as the Chief Minister that year and in 1974, she began her second term as Chief Minister. She left the office due to factionalism towards the end of 1976. In 1972, she won a prestigious by-election to the Orissa assembly from Cuttack. Among her contestants was late Biren Mitra, an Ex-Chief Minister of Orissa and long considered as the strongman of Cuttack politics. In 1974, she was elected from Dhenkanal assembly constituency. She retained that seat in both 1977 and 1980 with convincing margins. Mrs. Satpathy was regarded as the strong leader of Orissa politics. She had always been a hard fighter. No threats from the power center at Delhi controlled by Sanjay Gandhi frightened her. She would not succumb to threat. She was a strong administrator. Further, she was a great political strategist. She knows the strategy of alliance building. She proved very good in cultivating the right people at the right moment. Her political rise was quick and eye rising.

Apart from her political role, she has made a name as a progressive writer. She was particularly good in writing short stories. She was involved in many cultural activities. She attended the 15th General Conference of UNESCO at Paris as a member of the Indian delegation.

Sairindri Nayak

Sairindri Nayak, a Congress leader, belongs to Sambalpur district. Born in 1926 she was attracted towards politics. Since her student days, she took active part in the agitation, which was launched by the people of western Orissa against the construction of Hirakud Dam. This agitation, launched in early days of independence was regional in character. In other words, it was not organised in party line. Even though it was directed against the Congress government in Orissa. Many congress leaders of western Orissa supported it.

She was primary a schoolteacher. She married to Sri Durga Prasad Nayak, a lecturer in commerce. She had a long innings as a councilor of Sambalpur Municipality. She dominated the municipal politics of the town from 1950 to 1969. She was connected with associations and federations cultural as well as political.

She was the president of Sambalpur District Primary Teachers Federation for long 13 years. She was a member of the management of several colleges and high schools of Sambalpur district. She was a member of the senate and the syndicate of Sambalpur University from 1974 to 1977. Mrs. Nayak was also actively involved in labour politics. She was one of the important office bearers of Hirakud Industrial Workers Labour Union and Bhaskar Textiles Labour Union. She was the Vice-President of Sambalpur District Red Cross Society.

The political career of Mrs. Nayak took an important turn when she was elected to the Orissa Legislative Assembly on Congress ticket from Jharsuguda in 1974. After 3 years, she was re-elected to the Assembly from the same constituency. She took active part in the dissuasion on the floor of the Assembly. It was to her credit that she able to retain her seat in 1977 in spite of the Janata wave. However, in 1980, after having failed to get the Congress ticket, she contested as an independent and lost the election.

Saraswati Pardhan

Saraswati Pardhan belongs to a peasant caste of Sambalpur district. She was born in a middle-class family in 1975, and after getting higher education, she joined as a teacher in high school. However, after a few years she was attracted towards politics and joined the Indian National Congress in 1957. In 1961, she was elected to the Orissa Legislative Assembly on the Congress ticket and was appointed as a Deputy Minister, Education and remained in that post until 1967. In 1972, she was elected to the Rajya Sabha, until today she is continuing as an active member of the Congress party. In addition to her role in power politics, she has also been involved with the educational development of the state. For sometime, she was a member of the Sambalpur University Senate. Ms. Pradhan in spite of her long political career continues to be simple and unassuming. She lacks aggressiveness on what is known as "Kill instinct" for which she could not use much in power politics.

Rasa Manjari Devi

Rasa Manjari Devi, born in 1927 is the wife of Raja Bhajanaja Singh Deo of Tigiria of Cuttack district. Like many other ex-feudal lords, the Tigiria ruling family was attracted towards the Ganatantra Parishad and later the Swatantra Party. She is one of the few ex-queens of Orissa who joined power politics, which requires hand fight and tussle. She joined the Swatantra Party in 1967 and soon after this; she sought to capture the local power structure. Her first target was the Tigiria Panchayat Samiti. She was the Chairman of this Samiti from 1971 to 1974. In 1977 on the Janata ticket, she was elected to the Orissa Legislative Assembly.

Satyabhama Devi

Satyabhama Devi born in 1930, get married to Muralidhar Jena who was an honest politician and social worker of Balasore district. She extended her support to her husband in his social and political activities. After his death, she presumed by her well-wishers to join active politics. In 1977 on the Janata ticket, she was elected to the Orissa Legislative Assembly.

Ananda Manjari Devi

Kshatriya by caste, Ananda Manjari Devi was born in the ruling family of Palalahada of Dehenkanal district in 1925 and got married to the prince of Sukinda of Cuttack district. Her husband was Pitamber Hari Chandan Mahapatra. First, she was elected to the Orissa Legislative Assembly in 1961 as a Congress candidate. After the formation of Jana Congress, she joined it, thus cutting of her relation with the Congress. In 1977 on the Janata ticket, she won the Assembly election from Sukinda. Thus, she is one of the few Oriya women who have become MLA more than once. Moreover, she was one of the few ex-queens who initially preferred the Congress party to the Ganatantra Parishad, which was the first choice of most of the ex-rulers of the state. This shows that she is capable of taking independent, bold and unorthodox decisions.

Sudhansu Nalini Ray

Daughter of an eminent man, Lal Mohan Pattnaik, Sudhansu Nalini Ray was born in 1925. Her husband was late Brig S.K. Ray. Since her childhood, she was attracted towards public activities. Her father was great influence upon her. Highly educated and modernised Mrs. Ray joined the Congress Party in 1974.

She was elected to the Orissa Legislative Assembly from Gobindapur constituency of Cuttack district. She was the Chairman of the Sate Social Welfare Board.

Kiran Lekha Mohanty

Kiran Lekha Mohanty is an abrupt political leader. She has been in public life since long .Born in 1926, she joined Gandhian Institute for Rural Re-construction at Sevagram for education and training. She left the school in 1942 and as many other patriotic women joined the Quit India Movement for which she was kept in jail for more than 2 years. In 1945, she started an institution at Angul, namely Baji Raut Chatrabas, mainly for Advasi boys and girls. For a long time, she was an active worker in the Sarvodaya

Movement. During this phase, she was a close colleague of Malati Choudhury. First, she was a member of the Congress Party. But in 1957 she left that party and devoted herself to the Sarvodaya activists. She also actively participated in the total revolution of Jaya Prakash Narayan. In 1977, she was elected to the Orissa Legislative Assembly, on the Janata ticket.

V. Sugyani Kumari Deo

Sugyani Kumari by marriage is an Oriya. She was born in a feudal family at Madras in 1937 and got married to P.C. Mardaraj Deo, son of late Harihar Mardaraj, the ex-zamindar of Khallikote. The rulling family of Khalikote is politically well known. It played a leading role in the movement for the creation of Orissa as a separate state. Incidentally, the first meeting of Utkal Sammalani was held at Rambha, which was another palace of Khallikote zamindari. Moreover, in the post independence period, Harihar Mardaraj was attracted towards the active power politics. He was a minister for some time. This background of the Khallikote ruling family was apparently an asset to the political ambition of Sugyani Kumari, the daughter-in-law of great Harihar Mardaraj. She was not able to speak Oriya when she got married. However, in course of time, she could speak Oriya.

The above discussions show that women who have made their way to assembly had political background, educationally and economically well up and had record of social service. Some of them from the reserved constituencies also had the same background but had the additional benefit of reservation.

Constitutional Provisions for Women's Political Participation

The Constitution of India has granted equal political rights to all the citizens. However, in view of women's low entry into the Legislature, provision for reservation has been made in the local government institutions.

The Indian leaders have already felt this and reservation, even if it is 50 per cent, necessary to reach equality. Already one/third seats have been kept reserved for women in the Panchayat Raj Institutions and the proposed 81st amendment bill would enable Indian women to have 33 per cent reservation in the

Lok Sabha and in the state legislature. However, most of the major political parties like BJP and the Congress, the Janata Dal and the CPI (M) have promised 33 per cent reservation for women in their election manifestos, still there has been considerable tension over the bill.

Women constitute roughly half of the world's population. However, they are the largest excluded category in almost all respects. They have only 1/10th of the global income. They own 1/100th of the means of production. Nearly 70 per cent of the women live below the poverty line. 2/3rd of them are illiterate. They constitute almost invariably a small minority in respect of holding elected offices. In 1980, they made up of just over 10 per cent of the world's parliamentarians. The figure rose to 14.8 per cent in 1988 and it come down to 12.7 per cent in 1999.

The question of women's participation in politics assumed special importance only since 1975 when the United Nations declared the decade as the women development decade and adopted some resolutions for empowerment of women. The Nairobi Conference held in 1985 called on the participating countries to take steps for ensuring women's participation in politics through reservation of 35 per cent seats in all election.

Comparison of 81st Amendment and 84th Amendment for Women

81st Amendment

1. Minimum of 1/3 seat reserved for women in the Lok Sabha and Legislative Assembly;
2. Indefinite period of reservation;
3. Constituency reserved through draw of lots;
4. Reservation for women within the SC/ST quota. That is existing 22.5 per cent reserved for them and 7.5 per cent set aside for women.

Pros and Cons

1. After 50 years of independence women parliamentarians form not even 10 per cent of the total;
2. Reservations will give women the opportunity to gain political experience;

3. Reservation for women in Rajya Sabha and legislative council were not included;
4. Rotation of reserved seats will be deleterious to building accountability and responsibility of candidates (both men and women) to the constituencies;
5. As a result, the bibi-beti-brigade of male politicians will be installed in the reserved seats;
6. Women will not be given general tickets;
7. Women will only be contesting each other.

84th Amendment

It contains core provisions (and most of the pros and cons) as the 81st amendment with the following modifications:

1. Reservation of seats would only for fifteen years (three-five years term). After this period, there would be review;
2. Reservations for women in Rajya Sabha and Legislative Council will be included.

In order that the benefits of reservation are uniformly extended to SC/STs, There would be reservation for women. The modality is in the case of two seats, the first term the first seat is reserved and the 3rd term both the seats are general.

Similar provision has been made in case of states and Union Territories, which have one or two seats in Lok Sabha *i.e.* one of the 3-5 years term(fifteen year) would be reserved.

Pros and Cons

1. A review after fifteen years is more acceptable than reservations for an unlimited period;
2. Fine tuning of sub-reservations for SC/STs as well as for smaller states and Union Territories;
3. The Law Ministry stated that sub-reservation for OBCs and Muslim women are not legally tenable unless there was general reservation for OBC and Muslims. However, if there were general reservation for OBC and Muslims it would bring up the question of 50 per cent

casting limit on reservation seats, by the Supreme Court. Demand for sub-reservations to redress the political, economic and social imbalance;

4. OBC reservations would require demographic surveys. The OBC population is different in each state, with different states level.

Article 243 T (2) provides that not less than one third of the total number of seats reserved under clause (1) shall be reserved for women belonging to Scheduled Castes or as the case may be, the Scheduled Tribes. Clause (3) of the same article provides that "Not less than one-third (including the number of seats reserved for women belonging to Scheduled Castes and Scheduled Tribes) of the total number of seats to be filled by direct election in every municipality shall be reserved for women and such seats may be allotted by rotation to different constituencies in a municipality. Clause (4) of the above article provides that "the office of Chairperson in the Municipalities shall be reserved for the Scheduled Castes, Scheduled Tribes and women in such a manner as the legislature of a state may by law provide".

It has been noticed that after the amendment came into effect, the number of women contestants' are in the rural as well as in urban areas has increased.

Summary and Conclusion

Orissa is one of the poorest states in India with a semi feudal economy and a predominantly conservative culture. All through our history, the man has taken the central stage. The men who have by long traditions, forced women to remain under purda have mostly dominated the leadership and authority structures.

The emergence of the Oriya women in the struggle for India's freedom was an sensational episode. Their burning patriotism, supreme valour and gifted organisational abilities are written in the letters of gold in the history of Indian Freedom Movement.

Labanya Devi, the wife of Loknath Bahadur of Puri founded a women's association at Puri called "Mahila Bandhu Samiti". It had the primary membership of a few prominent women from the elite classes involved exclusively in the literary activities of women. This association provided impetus to women's talent and activity. In March 1921, Mahatma Gandhi addressed a small gathering of women at Vinod Vihari, Cuttack. Towards the end of 1921, Sarala Devi, with her husband joined active politics against the Pro-British Zamindar as well British authorities.Rama Devi, wife of Gopabandhu Choudhury, Hiramani Devi (mother of Niranjan Patnaik, an eminent Congress man of Ganjam), attended the Gaya session of the Indian National Congress held in 1922. The Calcutta session of the National Congress held in December 1928 was attended by Rama Devi, Sarala Devi, Sarojini Choudhury (daughter of Fakir Mohan Senapati), Jahnavi Devi and Kokila Devi.

The famous Salt Satyagraha in the year 1930 involved hundreds of women activists like Sarala Devi, Kishorimani Devi, Malati Devi, who came out from the seclusion of their homes to join Congress demonstrations for manufacturing salt. As soon as the Salt Satyagraha started at Inchudi, Rama Devi accompanied by Malati Devi, Annapurna Devi and Kiranabala Sen reached the Satyagraha center and violated the salt law camp at Balasore. Hundreds of women came under their amazing enthuse and leadership. On 20 April 1930, they led a long procession of women to the Satyagraha center and violated the salt law. Rama Devi, Annapurna Devi, Malati Devi and other women volunteers visited Srijang and encouraged the womenfolk of that area for violating salt law. Many Oriya women also took active part in preparing salt at different centers like Tandra, Bata, Inchudi, Kuanpur, Koligaon, Rasulpur and Kasha.

The involvement of Rani Bhagyabati Pattamahadei of Kujang in the Salt Satyagraha drew special attention. Thwarting the vigilance of one magistrate and the police party, Rani Pattamahadei, Rama Devi, and many other volunteers crossed to Kalia pata in a boat during dark hours of the night. Hundreds of women following the idea of their patriotic, Rani came forward to prepare contraband salt.

In the district of Ganjam, under the leadership of Sarala Devi, Malati Devi and others the salt "campaign took" the shape of a mass upsurge. Sarala Devi and Malati Devi made intensive tour and preached the morals of Satyagraha in the minds of women-folk throughout Ganjam area. About one fourth of the participants were women who willingly joined the struggle.

The political activities of the Oriya women reached its climax during the period of the Quit India Movement.Eminent women like Malati Choudhury, Rama Devi, Sarala Devi, Annapurna Maharana, and Mangala Devi, Subramanian Devi, Guan Manjari Devi, Champak Devi, Pravabati Devi, Sita Devi, Laxmi Bai and other contributed immensely in making the Quit India Movement a grand success.

It is important to note that even among the scheduled caste and scheduled tribe women, there were some freedom fighters. In the district hills of Koraput and Ganjam some tribal women raised their voices by jumping into the freedom struggle. History hardly recorded their great sacrifice. However, this would not minimise the magnitude of their sacrifices for the independence of their motherland.

After India became independent, there was some increase in the political participation of women. Some women contested in local and general elections. Few of them were appointed as Ministers both in states and in centre. However, the real power rested with man. It is true that Mrs. Gandhi played a long duration as the Prime Minister of India. Her elevation as the Prime Minister of India was mainly for the reason that she was the daughter of Jawaharlal Nehru, the most vital political leader of free India. Thus, the political ascendancy of Mrs. Gandhi does not really signify any general improvement in the political status of Indian women.

In Orissa a few women have became ministers. However, they were not very prominent up to the end of 1960. Male leaders like H.K. Mahatab, Biju Patnaik, R.N. Singh Deo and Biren Mitra dominated the political scene of Orissa. It is only in the 1970s that the political balance began to favour the women. Mrs. Nandini Satpathy who was Minister of State at the Center in the Indira Gandi's Cabinet was brought to Orissa as the Chief Minister in 1972. She remained as the chief Minister of Orissa up to 1976. She was an effective administrator and strong politician. Mrs. Satpathy who was a close match for male political actors of the state was forced to resign in 1976 and since then she has enthused in political uncertain. Although she dominated the political scene of Orissa for five years, her political supremacy did not signify any significant women power in Orissa politics.

After she was thrown out of power, no other Oriya woman could active and prominent in the state politics or in the national. It may be appropriately pointed out that, political participation of women in Orissa is more in upper politics than in local politics. Proportionately women figure in large number during Assembly and Lok Sabha election than in Panchayat Elections.

A closer look at these phenomena would suggest that the women who contest in general elections normally belong to higher middle castes, upper class, educated and progressive families. On the other hand, the social customs of the village greatly discourage women to take part in local politics and contest in Panchayat and Cooperative elections because villages are their main arms of politics. It is not a great surprise to take notice of the fact that there are many districts in Orissa without women Sarapanch before 73rd Amendment.

Findings

The sample survey indicates that the political modernisation of women is very poor. This is mainly due to their poverty, illiteracy and conservatism. There is hardly any discussion among family members or among the village women about politics.They discusses social matters and social issues of the villages. Similarly, the women are very poor in respect of reading newspapers and listening to radio or on news bulletin. Only exceptionally little quantity of them discuss politics or read about politics. Further the conservative culture of Orissa; greatly discourage the women to join politics. It is a social taboo for them. The people disrespect women moving freely with men in political organisations and forums. Thus, the political socialization as well as the political recruitment of Orissa women is very trivial.

It is interesting to observe that political participation in terms of political requirement confined to the woman of high status and women of low status are the women are deprived from it. Some female members belonging to higher castes like Brahmin, Karan and Kshatriyas have been elected to political posts to the Panchayats, to the assembly and to the parliament. Some of the scheduled castes and scheduled tribes women elected as MLAs and MPs because of the reservations. It is pertinent to note that the election success of scheduled caste or scheduled tribe women is merely symbolic. They are just "token elites" with out exercising any power and hardly being considered by other as influential.

A large number of women go to the polling booths and cast their votes. In terms of voting, their record is impressive. However, they did not give their votes according their choice. They just vote as advised and instructed by her husband or another important member if it is a joint family.

There are only a very hardly any cases where the wives disagree from her husband regarding their electoral choice. The women are hardly seen active in organising party meetings taking part in political processions and organising political meetings. They do not go there on their own option. They predisposed by the male members of particular families to attend political meetings or take part in political procession. This shows that the political participation is awfully insignificant in the area of study.

REFERENCES

Secondary Sources

1. Baral J.K. and Jena B.B. – *Orissa Government and Politics*.
2. Bhambari C.P. and P.S. Verma – *The Urban Voters*, Delhi, 1973.
3. Carter Gwendolen M. – *Government and Politics*, 3rd Ed., New York.
4. Choudhury B.C. and Das H.H. – *Introduction to Political Sociology*, Vidyapuri Publications.
5. Fadia B.L. – *Indian Government and Politics*, Sahitya Bhawan, Agra 1996.
6. Gandhi M.K. – *M.K. Gandhi and Social Justice*, Bombay, 1947.
7. Gandhi M.K. – *The Role of Women, Bombay 1964*, Bharatiya Vidya Bhavan.
8. Gupta Giri Raj – *Family and Social Change in Modern India*, Vikash, New Delhi, 1976.
9. Hamanzeigen. L – *Introduction to Political Science, People Politics and Perception*, New Jersy Publications.
10. Panda Snehalata – *Empowerment of Women*.
11. Patnaik Sudhakar – *History of Freedom Movement in Orissa*, Cuttack – 1951, Vol. III.
12. Robert L. – Lineberry and Irashai Kansky – *Urban Politics and Public Policy*, New York Publications.

13. Veena Poonacha "*Gender with the Human Rights Discourse*" Published by SNDT University, Bombay, 1998.

14. Heldi Hammonton "*The Unhappy Marriage of Marxism and Feminism: Towards a Non-progressive Union*.

Weekly News

15. *Employment News* Dt. 24-30 June 2000, Political Empowerment of Women by Rashmi Thakur.

Journals and Magazines

16. *Census Report of India and Orissa* 2001.

17. *Economic and Political Weekly*, July 31st, 1999, Vol. XXV, No. 31.

18. Economic and Political Weekly, Jan. 9th, 1999, Vol. XXIV, Nos. 1 & 2

19. Gender Just Laws – 'Bulletin No.4, Dec. 1998.

20. *Kurukshetra*, 1995 to 2000.

21. *The M.M. Magazine*, Sept. 1997, Vol. IV, No. 7.

22. Mukhopadhya Anal Kumar, Political Sociology published on behalf of K.P. Bagchi and Co.

23. *Orissa Review*, Vol. IV, No. 7 & 8, Feb-March, 2000.

24. *Politics in India*, March 1999.

25. *Politics in India*, April 1998, Vol. II, No. 10.

26. *Who's Who in Lok Sabha* in 1952 to 1991.

27. *Who's Who in Rajya Sabha* in 1952 to 1991.

28. *Yojana*, Vol. 44, No. 2, Nov. 2000.

10

WOMEN'S PARTICIPATION IN PANCHAYATI RAJ INSTITUTIONS

Dr. GIRISH KUMAR DAS*

Political participation is the necessary ingredient of every political system. Political participation is the involvement of groups and individuals at various levels in the political system. According to Almond "It is the involvement of the members in the decision making process of the system. Political participation denotes a series of bearing on the political process that involves issues like the selection of the rulers and the various aspects of the formation of public policy. These activities mainly are: (a) voting at the pools; (b) supporting possible pressure groups by being a member of them; (c) personally communicating directly with the legislators; (d) participating in the political activity; (e) engaging in habitual dissemination of political opinions. Lestor Milbrath brings these activities under the following three categories: gladiatorial activities, transitional activities and spectacular activists. Gladiatorial activities includes a small number of party activities whose active association with political parties keep them engaged in a series of direct party activities like holding party offices, fighting the elections as party candidates, raising party funds, attending party meeting and joining the party campaigns.

* **Lecturer in Political Science, Kotpad College, Kotpad, Distt. Koraput, Orissa.**

Transitional activities includes attending party meetings as the supporters of the party, making contributions to the party funds and coming in contact with public officials or party personnel . Voting, influencing others in particular way, exposing oneself to political stimuli are the spectacular activities.

Provisions for Women in 73rd Constitutional Amendment and Orissa Gram Panchayat Act

(i) Not less than one-third of the seats meant for direct election of members at each their of Panchayats are to be reserved for the women;

(ii) Not less than one-third of the total number of reserved under clause (1)shall be reserved for women belonging to the Scheduled Castes or as the case may be, the Scheduled Tribes;

(iii) Not less than one-third (including the number of seats reserved for women belonging to the Scheduled Castes and Scheduled Tribes) of the total number of seats to be filled by the direct election in every Panchayat shall be reserved for women and such seats may be allotted by rotation to different constituencies in a Panchayat.;

(iv) Not less than one-third of the seats of chairperson at any level reserved for women.

There are some special provisions regarding the reservation of women in Orissa Panchayat Raj institutions.

Panchayati Raj Institutions, the grass root units of self-government have been proclaimed as the vehicles of socio-economic transformation in rural India. Effective and meaningful functioning of these bodies would depend on active involvement, contribution and participation of its citizens both male and female. For women sharing of power on equal terms with men should be the major strategy so that they can play an effective role in the decision making process.

The words 'grass root' has mutually reinforcing economic, political and geographical connotations. In the context of the current Indian women's movement such a focus seems to be appropriate as the maximum emphasis has been placed on the empowerment of women at the grass root to the poor women in rural and urban areas.

The committee on Panchayati Raj Structures (1977-78) emphasised the need for village level women's organisation to influence both the directional and implementation levels of development planning. The need to organise rural women workers to eliminate their economic and social vulnerability was emphasised not only by the policy making bodies of this country out by the Non Aligned Movement (Baghdad 1979) and United Nations system as well by the mid eighties *e.g.*, Copenhagen Programme of Action.

The women's movement in this country also realized at the same time that in certain context it would be difficult to claim exclusive women's rights and therefore it would be best to penetrate such areas through representation in Panchayati Raj Institutions.

Women's participation in setting the agenda for their own and others development and not merely to get on to such agenda requires immediate action. This would require women's empowerment. At the same time such an empowerment can come to women only with their socio-political advancement and an increase in their number and participation in decision making on the other.

One level of understanding women's participation both as voters and candidates (wherever elections have been held) for the Panchayati Raj Institutions is at grass root level. The one important theme on which the recent debates on Panchayati Raj seems to be involving around is the participation of women in Panchayati Raj Institutions. Such a participation, in turn has been dealt with at two levels, namely (i) the representation of women in the Panchayati Raj Institutions either as members or as functionaries and (ii) the substance and effectiveness of such representation.

In the beginning when Panchayati Raj was introduced in India in 1959, very few women contested or got elected. The Balvantrai Meheta Committee 1957 had recommended that besides the 20 members of the Panchayat Samiti, there should be two women "who are interested in work among women and children" as co-opted members. Following this a few states did make provisions for women's representations.

Now that in Panchayats one third representation of women is operational in most of India and similar representations of women is imminent in state Assemblies and Parliament. It is necessary to formulate a comprehensive programmme of training in order to enable women to play their part fully and effectively in our democracy.

To be accepted and looked up to as representatives of the whole people, women panchayat members should first of all be able to articulate and espouse the common problems of the village, block, district or the Assembly and the Parliamentary constituency also the nation as a whole as the case may be.

Regarding the 73rd constitutional amendment and its implications for women, scholars believe that through this Amendment the country has passed from democracy by consent to democracy by participation. It restores power to people to whom it belongs. The women who enter public life are relatives (wives; sisters, etc.) of male public figures and more often than not act as directed by them . Often they degenerate into party spokesmen and hardly voice their own opinion on the floor of the house. Most of them remain as silent spectators to the proceedings of the house.

Women have to improve themselves through education, take an interest in public and social affairs and become popular leaders themselves. It is imperative that they came up by their own and not with the help of their male relatives. Only they can stand up for the problem of the people in general and women in particular. Panchayati Raj Institutions, are, in fact considered to be the most effective instruments for realising the goals of economic betterment and social justice for the least privileged. Participation of women in Panchayati Raj has been considered essential for enabling them to participate effectively and independently in democratic and political process and to influence decision making. It has been recognised as a step towards equal society and a means of realising the development goals for women.

The introduction of women's organisation and the consequent emergence of women leadership at the grass root level has brought about social changes in the rural women's life, In general and village communities in particular. The formal reservation of women in Panchayati Raj structures, through reservation of seats, election etc, is not a sufficient condition for their effective participation unless and until it is supplemented by measures which help in solving the socio-economic pressures inhibiting them. The same can be realised by mobilising women through awareness campaign and interpersonal communication by implementing the scheme witch help them in attaining economic independence and by enhancing educational facilities at their door step.

REFERENCES

1. Milbarth .L, *Political Participation,* Rand M C Nally, Chicago, 1985.
2. Government of India (1977-78) *Report of the Committee on Panchayati Raj.*
3. Kausik Susheela, *Women and Panchayati Raj.*
4. Usha Narayanan, *Women in Panchayats, The Path Head In*, Mainstream, Vol. xxxiv, 1996.
5. Das Hari Hara, *Introduction to Panchayat Raj and Community Development in India*, Kalyani Publishers, New Delhi-1990.

Index

Z

❑❑❑